W9-BEC-089

The Tao of Sales

The Tao of Sales

The Easy Way
to Sell in Tough Times

E. Thomas Behr, Ph.D.

ELEMENT
Shaftesbury, Dorset • Rockport, Massachusetts
Brisbane, Queensland

© Element Books, Inc., 1997
Text © E. Thomas Behr, 1997

First published in the USA in 1997 by
Element Books, Inc.
21 Broadway, Rockport, MA 01966

Published Great Britain in 1997 by
Element Books Limited
Shaftesbury, Dorset SP7 8BP

Published in Australia in 1997 by
Element Books Limited for
Jacaranda Wiley Limited
33 Park Road, Milton, Brisbane 4064

All rights reserved. No part of this book may be reproduced or utilized,
in any form or by any means, electronic or mechanical, without prior
permission in writing from the Publisher.

Library of Congress Cataloging-in-Publication Data
Behr, E. Thomas, 1940-
The tao of sales: the easy way to sell in tough times.
/ E. Thomas Behr.—1st ed.
p. cm.
Includes bibliographical references.

British Library Cataloguing in Publication data available

Back cover photograph © 1997 Mary E. Behr.
Cover design by Foster & Foster
Text design by Kathryn Sky-Peck
Typeset in 11.5 Garamond with Diotima display
Printed and bound in the USA by Courier Westford
ISBN 1-86204-058-3

First Edition
10 9 8 7 6 5 4 3 2 1

For information about the book, or questions about training programs related to the
Tao of Sales, please contact E. Thomas Behr, (908) 647-6489, or
EthomasB@AOL.COM

*Figure on page 138 is Copyright © 1992 by The Traditional Acupuncture Institute, Inc. All
rights reserved. Permission to reproduce this diagram in any form or by any means must be
obtained from The Traditional Acupuncture Institute, American City Building, Suite 100,
Columbia, MD. (301) 596-6606. For information about their programs for laypersons in
Philosophy and Healing in Action, call Maryanne Blair, (410) 997-4888.*

CONTENTS

I have three treasures:
simplicity, patience, and compassion.

Tao Te Ching 67

To Jenny, thank you for the gift of simplicity.
To Mary, thank you for the gift of patience.
To JoAnn, thank you for the gift of compassion.

ACKNOWLEDGMENTS

OF THE MANY CONSULTANTS, salespeople, sales managers, and sales trainers I have worked with, I would especially like to thank the following for their contributions to my understanding of the "art" of selling and service: Vince Agnew, Lauren Anderson, Tita Beal, Peter Block, Kathy Boyle, Candace Deasy, Shari Ford, Paul Gravél, Burton Hall, David Haapaoja, Leslie Holleran, John Hone, Mel Kosko, Joe Masterson, Maria Montoya, Roz Parry, Linda Price, Susan Rosner, Steve Smith, Barbara Szala, Greg Turner, and Carlos Valdez-DaPena.

I wrote the first draft of this book during a period of intensive sales training and consulting with PR Newswire, when they were making a total organizational (and personal) commitment to becoming a value-added service "champion." Thanks to their entire sales staff for being my "teachers," and to their Executive Committee for helping me through some tough times when I wrestled with the pressure of confronting a client's organizational change while keeping a clear focus on what was really important to them: the growth and development of people.

Joseph and Carolyn Borlo started me out in the discovery of Zen thinking and Zen space, and continue to bring joy to our friendship.

Joe Masterson, Tom Vietorisz, John Gillespie, JoAnn, Mary, and Jenny Behr read this manuscript in its various forms (many of them rough drafts, indeed), and provided both helpful feedback and needed encouragement. Special thanks to Peter Behr, an editor/senior reporter with the *Washington Post*, for demanding that I be clear and focused. Every writer needs the critical discipline of a tough editor. I suspect few writers have received criticism in so caring a manner. Melody McMahon labored over the manuscript with her characteristic great patience and loving, extraordinary attention to detail.

Scott Pfluger of PriorGraphics contributed to both the spirit and creativity of this book, as he does with all his clients, and helped to maximize artistic quality and cost-effectiveness. His questions and insights into the changing nature of marketing also contributed to several sections of this book.

Joe Westfield, of Dash Offset, has handled our various printing needs for years, and in so doing has created his own definition of what superior service is all about.

Kathryn Sky-Peck edited and designed this book with a sensitive artist's awareness of the "sculpture within the stone"—always responsive to the intent of my language and the much deeper resonance of the Tao itself which that language sought to evoke.

Final thanks to Del Riddle, Roberta Scimone, and Jennifer Collins of Element Books for believing so strongly in this project, for their professional insight and personal support, and their willingness to work with me in a spirit of partnership that embodies all the virtues of *The Tao of Sales*.

The Master always "teaches" without teaching.

A GUIDE FOR THE READER

THE TAO OF SALES takes the commonly recognized 81 verses of the *Tao Te Ching* and groups them in seven thematic sections as shown in the table of contents, each section with its own theme. Each section has ten chapters, each chapter representing a verse from the *Tao Te Ching*. The book concludes with a coda of 11 verses as a summary. Each chapter of the *Tao of Sales* starts with my meditation on the original Tao, and focuses on a specific application to selling in today's world.

The last section of *The Tao of Sales*, "Simple Selling," describes a sales process that integrates all the techniques and insights of the separate chapters.

Interspersed throughout the book, indicated by the Chinese character for Tao, 道, are discussions on Taoism as it relates to today's world. At the bottom of each of the chapters is a daily action step designed to help you act on the insights contained within that page. I have identified these by the Chinese symbol for "Te," or "virtue," 德 . When thinking about Taoist "virtue," it helps to remember, as Alan Watts has pointed out, that it means "...virtue not in the sense of moral propriety, but virtue in the sense of magic, as when we speak of the healing virtues of a certain plant." The first definition of "virtue" is exclusive, and divides us from other people and all creation. The second is inclusive, allowing us to share in the "wholeness" of people and events.

"But suppose I want to skip all the mushy stuff and just get to the good parts?"

Each group of seven chapters is followed by a specific list of practice exercises—what other sales books might call "techniques." It's possible to just skip to those sections, find actions that make sense to you, practice those actions mindfully, and pay attention to what happens. The trick is the word "mindfully." Almost any technique used simply, compassionately, and patiently, for healthy purposes, will "work." No technique, used for unhealthy purposes, will produce anything other than frustration and pain.

If the reader wishes, it is possible to move through the *Tao of Sales* a week at a time, working with each of the seven groups of chapters, and the section of "how to" suggestions at the end of each group. Or follow any other path that seems helpful.

The real exercise, of course, is to read the *Tao Te Ching* itself. Nothing replaces that. Within the text, I have indicated the various translators of passages I have quoted. Full references are provided in the Notes section beginning on page 143. Where no author is cited, the version is mine.

A TRUE STORY

I WAS RECENTLY SITTING in my dentist's office uncharacteristically early for my appointment. In through the door walked a young, eager, freshly-scrubbed sales rep, instantly identifiable by the detail bag and the hurried, pre-call anxiety. As she walked in, I was struck by how frantic she was, and how oblivious to everything around her. She straightened her clothing, fumbled in her bag for a business card, sighed, and approached the receptionist, slapping a cheery smile on her face as she went. There could have been no one else in the room.

Her bright "Hi, I'm — from — . Does the doctor have a few moments to talk?" was dashed by the receptionist.

"Do you have an appointment?" the receptionist asked.

"No," was the answer, "but I wonder if the doctor could give me a few minutes. I'm from — and we're the largest manufacturer of…"

The receptionist cut the rep off. "I know who you are. The doctor's very busy. I'll see if he can give you some time." The rep sat down next to me.

"So," I said. "A sales rep, huh? I spotted you the moment I saw the bag. What do you sell?" Happy to be given a chance to talk, the rep told me. Some time later, when I asked about the rep's territory, I learned that her mission was to get products in front of dentists, working off a prospect base of roughly 2,000.

"It must be tough to get the dentist's time," I volunteered. "After all, you're taking them away from the two things they care most about—treating their patients and earning money. And you're asking them to spend their most precious assets: their knowledge and their time. The more successful the dentist, the less time they have to see any rep. What would happen if you called for an appointment?"

"Oh no. We're supposed to knock on doors and get them interested in our new products. It's all about…" (She quoted from one of those "You can become wealthy if you sacrifice enough" books.) I decided to leave sales efficiency, planning, and territory management alone and try selling skills.

"So what do you have to show him?"

I got a great demonstration of a new syringeable hybrid composite that combines strength with fluoride release. "But suppose he's not interested in that?" I asked. "How do you find out what he's really interested in?"

"I know I'm supposed to ask questions but when there's so little time, it's easier to try to get him hooked on the product."

I said, "It must be tough under time pressure to get him to really listen to what you're saying. How do you 'bait' your hook?"

"It's hard," she responded. "They really are too busy to listen. But I just have to try harder." She seemed convinced and determined, at least for that moment. Probably had been listening to the tape in her car—the one that says: "Your primary tool—the opening in your face called a mouth—must be used with confidence."

I was called in for my appointment with the assistant. Fifteen minutes later, the doctor joined us, having spent five minutes with the rep. "How did it go with the rep?" I asked.

"I like to give them a little time because I know they have a job to do, but somebody ought to teach these reps how to call on doctors," he said. "No appointment. That wastes my time and the rep's.

"All the rep did was pitch a product at me without finding out what I need. Then she tried to sell the benefits. That's just dumb. I don't make decisions that might affect patient health and the quality of my work just based on a sales endorsement or marketing materials. I check it out with CRA in Provo, Utah. I know they're unbiased. A lot of dentists would have thrown the rep out of the office."

———————

THIS BOOK WILL NOT, BY ITSELF, make you richer, more successful, happier, less stressed-out, or more in control of your life and future. You have to do that for yourself.

What this book can do is:

- Help you change how you sell and why you sell so that the process becomes easier, for you and your customers or clients.
- Help you focus your sales efforts on value—the value you create in yourself and share with others.
- Help you add value to what you offer clients and customers, and get that added value back in bigger, better sales.
- Show you how to prioritize your time and efforts with those clients and customers who meet you more than half-way.
- Allow you to achieve goals by collaborating with customers and clients, instead of fighting against them or trying to use them just to get what you want.
- Allow you to flow with resistance, frustration, doubt, and setbacks, like water going down hill, instead of getting trapped in negative feelings, actions, and outcomes.
- Help you build "championship" sales teams by working on the actions that create results, instead of simply trying to manage the results themselves.
- Enable you to build a stronger, "value-based" entrepreneurial business.
- Allow you to integrate purpose, joy, and accomplishment in your professional and personal lives.

Selling the easy way: Doing things with customers, instead of to them, or even for them.

PREFACE

ONE "SOURCE" OF *The Tao of Sales* comes from outside the boundaries of conventional American thought, in the *Tao Te Ching*, a philosophical and spiritual Chinese text attributed to a rather elusive sage, Lao Tzu.

This is a personal response to the *Tao Te Ching*, not a translation. In shaping that response I have been allowing my thoughts to bounce off and grow out of John Heider's book, *The Tao of Leadership*, and the translations of the *Tao Te Ching* by Thomas Cleary, Gia-Fu Feng and Jane English, D.C. Lau, Robert G. Henricks, Man-Ho Kwok, Martin Palmer and Jack Ramsay, and Stephen Mitchell. Cleary's translation of Chuang Tzu and of the very Taoist *The Art of War*, by Sun Tzu, have also been valuable sources. Paul Reps' *Zen Flesh, Zen Bones*, and Thich Nhat Hanh's *Peace is Every Step,* and the writings of Alan Watts have long been friends, comforting at times, demanding at others. When I needed a break, or a reminder of the value of Taoist laughter, I read *The Tao of Meow*, translated by Carl Japiske. When I thought I was taking this all too seriously, I went back to Benjamin Hoff's *The Tao of Pooh* and *The Te of Piglet*. In understanding the Taoist awareness of the universe, Fritjof Capra's *The Tao of Physics*, Gary Zukav's *The Dancing Wu Li Masters*, and Margaret Wheatley's *Leadership and the New Science* have been stimulating, sometimes puzzling, but always insightful.

A second source consists of the thousands of salespeople, managers, and executives I've worked with as a consultant and salesperson over the past 15 years. It reflects their successes and frustrations, their fears, and most important, their hopes.

A third source is the 1735-vintage farm on ten acres along a peaceful river that JoAnn and I were led to by serendipity, or some even higher power; we certainly didn't deserve it or intend ever to be here. It's on loan to us.

Anyone who knows old houses will recognize that Thoreau was right, we don't own our houses, they own us. But there's peaceful discipline in working with walls out of plumb, floors that aren't level, plaster that's turned to cement, and foundations that want to return back to the earth from which they came.

There's another kind of joyful discipline in the passage of seasons painted across the hill above the river, in the arrivals and departures of hawks and geese, songbirds, wild turkeys, and great blue heron. We share our lives gratefully with untamed deer and our equally untamed dairy goats, and work to keep from sharing JoAnn's herb and vegetable gardens with them, too. If I have written well, some of that peacefulness lives in these pages.

A Personal Journey

A master was asked the question, "What is the Way?" by a curious monk.

"It is right before your eyes," said the master.

"Why do I not see it for myself?"

"Because you are thinking of yourself."

"What about you: do you see it?"

"So long as you see double, saying I don't and you do, and so on, your eyes are clouded," said the master.

"When there is neither 'I' nor 'You,' can one see it?"

"When there is neither 'I' nor 'You,' who is the one that wants to see it?"

THIS IS A BOOK ABOUT succeeding in a new, unfamiliar world, the customer-driven world of the future.

Because we can guess so little about how that future will actually evolve, it is also a book about transformations—changing how we think and feel and act, in response to and harmony with the changing times we live in.

It makes as much sense to say that the *Tao Te Ching* "chose" me as the model for this book as to say that I chose it. I encountered Jane English and Gia-Fu Feng's graceful translation and provocative photographs first in 1978, during a period of personal challenge and growth.

In the succeeding years, as I pursued a career change from education into business and began selling for my living, it stayed with me—not always present in the front of my mind, but still quietly there, like a neglected garden which one really intends to return to some day to re-cultivate. Meanwhile, deep inside, things kept growing in their own way and time.

In 1989, watching me struggle with a particularly difficult seminar group, Richard Thomas, then of Renaissance Leadership Inc., suggested I read John Heider's marvelous adaptation, *The Tao of Leadership*. I did, and that began a gradual transformation in my life and work that continues.

Around the same time, my colleagues and I began confronting a powerful set of changes in what we were experiencing from our own clients, changes echoed in the frustrations and difficulties experienced by the salespeople whom we were training and the customers they, themselves, served. Simply put, the old approaches to selling weren't working, and the latest books on selling weren't helping much either.

We found ourselves and our clients eagerly, even desperately, seeking stability and security in a world all of us recognized was spinning around us. Our clients wanted "safe" buying decisions; the executives, managers, and salespeople we worked with wanted simple answers and "surefire" techniques.

What we were overlooking was, in part, the very physics of change. If things are spinning around you, apparently out of control, then looking outside of one's self for stability means entering the dark, swirling edges of the storm. No stability there.

The New Physics tells us that what we call "reality" is our imperfect (and wishful) view of the chaos by which the physical world actually operates, and what we call "chaos" is our imperfect view of the deeper order that emerges, unpredictable and uncontrollable, out of the flow of events.

So one starts looking for balance instead of control; being calmly "centered" (like a gyroscope) rather than being forceful; acting truthfully instead of "safely." That search for balance, calm, and integrity has lead me into the investigation of my own spiritual values as the center of my actions with others. One of my guides during that journey has been the Tao, and the daily written meditations on selling that have resulted in this book.

I invite you to make your own journey through these pages.

You can expect it, at first, to be a strange, perhaps difficult, perhaps at times threatening journey, because to take the first step means moving beyond the comfortable limits we place around our lives.

> *When people see some things as beautiful,*
> *other things become ugly.*
> *When people see some things as good,*
> *other things become bad.*

For many of us, the sign on the boundary of those limits reads "Good Inside, Bad Outside." What we know, what we're familiar and comfortable with is "Good." The unknown, the unfamiliar, the very experience of change, is easily labeled "Bad—To be avoided." Because we like living in a coherent world, it's easy enough to label what we know as "rational," "sensible," "correct," and "moral" and all that stuff outside the boundaries as "irrational," "nonsense," "incorrect," and "immoral." (I think of all the times in seminars when participants, faced with a concept or behavior that lay beyond the comfort level of their experience, resisted change by saying "But you know, in the real world, we can't....") Is it possible that when we say "Good" and "Bad" we're meaning "Safe" and "Unsafe"?

Because it looks squarely at a dangerous world, the Tao is not safe.

> *Success is as dangerous as failure.*
> *Hope is as hollow as fear.*

If we are alert to what's happening in the world, we discover that things outside the boundaries of our experience and desires have their own uncomfortable reality. Try as we may, it's hard to make events work out as we wish.

We act in what we believe is a rational way only to be confronted by a larger "irrationality" that seems to care little, or not at all, for our carefully crafted plans.

If we merely redouble our efforts to make things work the way we want them, those efforts have a frustrating way of producing results exactly the opposite of what we wanted or expected. (I think of the salespeople and managers I know whose only answer to an unmanageable 60-hour work week is to put in longer hours doing the same things that make them crazy to begin with.)

> *Fill your bowl to the brim*
> *and it will spill.*
> *Keep sharpening your knife*
> *and it will blunt.*
> *Chase after money and security*
> *and your heart will never unclench.*

Because it deliberately steps away from a dangerous world, the Tao is not unsafe. The world seems complicated; the Tao is simple. Our thoughts and actions are superficial; the Tao is deep.

> *In dwelling, live to the ground.*
> *In thinking, keep to the simple.*
> *In conflict, be fair and generous.*
> *In governing, don't try to control.*
> *In work, do what you enjoy.*
> *In family life, be completely present.*

One way to begin a personal exploration of the Tao is to notice the difference between what it says and the values that drive your personal actions. For many salespeople, this difference has the force of conflict.

Control vs. Spontaneity

Traditional selling and sales management demand that we become experts at using power to control people, events, and outcomes. The Tao invites us to become masters of purposeful spontaneity.

One of the great gifts of the times we live in is the clarity of the message that control doesn't work. It doesn't work in selling, it doesn't work in business, it doesn't work in personal relationships. To set foot on the "way" of the Tao is to look that fact squarely in the eye.

"How can I stop trying to control things?" a client asked me. "I can't live with just letting things go wild around here. And my bosses expect me to exercise control. That's how I'm paid. That's how I keep my job."

"How safe really is your job?" I asked. "What kinds of results do you get from all that effort to manage things? Do you feel in control? Your feelings are sending you a strong message. What would happen if you listened to them?"

The message sent by our feelings is often one of change. "Stop doing what you're doing. Try something new." If we receive that message when we're frantic and not thinking clearly, however, we're likely to misinterpret it. Our inside wisdom speaks in a quiet voice; if we've tuned our hearing to the loud shouting of the world around us ("WORK HARDER!" "MAKE MORE SALES!" "REACH YOUR BUDGET OR ELSE!") we may miss the inner message completely. Even when we hear the message, we may resist letting go of the urge to control things. Because so much seems to be changing around us, we may want to cling to the apparent consistency of what we already know how to do.

It may help to understand that spontaneity is not the opposite of control. It means doing what you think is best in each situation. If it makes sense to dictate how things should be done, do it; if it makes sense to ask others what they think, do it. If it makes sense to push the relationship with a customer, do it; if it makes sense to allow the customer to take the lead, do it.

Say exactly what is needed in that moment and then be silent.
Do exactly what is needed in that moment and then be quiet.

What keeps us from exercising the freedom of spontaneity is fear. We fear that without control, we won't get what we want (or will get what we fear); we fear the loss of others' approval (and thus our own loneliness).

Fear vs. Trust

Fear starts early. "Don't play so near the steps! Don't run in the street! Don't play with fire! Don't talk to strangers!"

Sometimes the messages are disguised. "Don't disobey your parents, or disappoint us, or contradict us (or we'll stop loving you)." "Don't be 'different' (or other people will stop liking you)." "Don't take risks, or trust other people, or fight the system (or other people will start hurting you)."

We learn these lessons as children, and turn them into immutable laws as adults. In time they become the signs on the prison walls we construct around ourselves.

Parents need to decide for themselves whether fear is the best way to teach children to understand the consequences of their actions, or protect them when they aren't ready to understand. Letting a child play with matches or run uncontrolled into a busy street is both unloving and dumb. So is needlessly stifling a child's sense of wonder and discovery.

It's also unloving and dumb to treat adults as if they were still children— or treat ourselves that way.

Lacking the knowledge of consequences, a child is not able to choose. As adults we have both the knowledge and the freedom to choose. One might say we have the obligation to choose.

Some people spend their lives in fear of death, constantly seeking to avoid the inevitable. Some people spend their lives in fear of life, constantly missing the joy of what is possible.

Some people enjoy life while alive and don't fear death because until it happens they are still alive. Plenty of time to cope with death when we're dead.

Whatever we fear is waiting around the next corner each day of our journey through life. The less we fear, the more open and untroubled that road.

On your best, your happiest day, did you think about anything at all, or did you just experience that day in its fullness? Where was time then? Where was worry?

"My District Manager only cares about looking good and keeping her job," another client argued. "She'd sell any of us out in a heartbeat if she thought it would make her look good. And my Regional Manager's in a fog; he doesn't have a clue. He'd be calling room service on the Titanic to tidy up his stateroom as the ship was sinking.... How in the world can I trust them?"

"Whoever said trust and naiveté were synonyms?" I asked. "If they're harmful people, it makes sense to be thoughtful about how you deal with them. But I'm interested in how fear affects you. When fear is your primary motivator, how does that cause you to act? To think? To feel? What's the impact on people whom you might be able to trust? What do they see in you? I wonder if you come across just like your District and Regional Managers?"

> *"The sage is never opinionated,*
> *He listens to the mind of the people."*
> *I am kind to people when they are kind to me.*
> *I am kind to them even if they hate me.*
> *Virtue—te—is its own reward.*
> *I trust those who trust me,*
> *I also trust those who have no faith in me:*
> *What I give, I receive.*

If fear drives our actions, is it possible we're afraid to trust ourselves to act in honest, caring ways? Is it possible that we question others' integrity and intentions because we're not sure of our own?

Trust works when we reach out of ourselves. It is most powerful when we choose to trust during moments of greatest doubt.

Trust works when we reach deep inside of ourselves for what is best within us.

What is built on rock
　　　　cannot be pulled down
What is held lightly
　　　　can never be lost.
How can I see the world like this?
Because I have eyes.

Awareness vs. Knowledge

"If you ask me to trust," the same client continued, "you're asking me to let go of what I know about the world."

"Exactly," I replied. "You got it."

Knowledge is a way of exercising control. The more we "know," the more power we may feel over people who know "less." If we need to feel good about ourselves, we can use "superior" knowledge to make other people feel inferior. Knowledge allows us to escape making tough choices; we choose the "logical," "approved," "sensible" option because we "know" it's the right thing to do. We follow the rules, and when things go wrong, we blame the rules.

> *The Master sees things as they are,*
> *without trying to control them.*
> *She lets them go their own way,*
> *and resides at the center of the circle.*

Knowledge translates into processes and techniques—the right way of doing things: 14 Steps for total quality, 5 Steps for managing troubled employees, 8 Steps for managing projects, 10 Steps for developing high performance teams, 6 Steps for the perfect sales presentation. So many steps, so little real progress.

> *Clever people know how to manipulate things.*
> *Harmful people know how to manipulate other people.*
> *Wise people know merely themselves.*

Self-knowledge is awareness. Paying full attention to what's happening, free from the filters of expectations and fears, is awareness. That's enough to work with.

> *The mark of a moderate man*
> *is freedom from his own ideas.*

"Are you saying I should forget about planning?" a highly successful sales-man asked.

"Yes and no. The more you know about your own goals, needs, and fears, the better. The more you know about your customer's world, the better. The trick is to let go of the desire to control outcomes. If planning limits your ability to respond powerfully and wholly to the situation facing you and the customer, it's worse than useless."

"But what about technique? I rely on it. Without what I've learned how to do, I'm helpless."

"Same answer. We've both seen salespeople blow calls because they were so intent on doing things the right way that they never got around to doing the right thing. If you're aware of what's happening, you'll know what to do in that moment. Without awareness, no technique in the world works. If you trust enough to act decisively in each moment, you don't need control."

> *Technique and wisdom. Technique is "male," powerful, intrusive, commanding, rational. Wisdom is "female," enduring, encompassing, flowing, intuitive. That is why the masters knew the technique but followed wisdom.*
>
> *Technique seeks to change things, wisdom to be at one with them as they evolve. Technique is personal, and says to the world, "Obey me." Wisdom is impersonal, and allows the world to be what it is.*

If we come from a Western culture, especially American, we may well approach the Tao in terms of contradictions and conflict: Fear vs. Trust, Control vs. Spontaneity, Knowledge vs. Awareness. Which should I choose? What's the right way to do things? What happens if I guess wrong? In today's world we are likely to feel like the character in Gary Larson's Far Side cartoon, standing before two doors in Hell, being prodded by the Devil to make a choice. One door says "Damned if You Do." The other says "Damned if You Don't."

It is said that we learn contradiction and conflict at birth, at the moment of separation when we enter the world, and all through the stage of infancy in which we are helplessly dependent on our parents for all our needs. We want both the sense of union and unconditional love and, at the same time, our own unique individuality. How do I assert my separate self without denying my bond with others? How do I become one with another person without losing my own uniqueness? That conflict plays itself out in all our relationships: parents and children, lovers and friends, wives and husbands, bosses and subordinates, salespeople and customers. The contradiction we feel is between dominance and dependency. Choose dominance and we forfeit love; choose dependency and we lose self-respect. "Damned if You Do, Damned if You Don't."

But contradiction and conflict are only the appearance of things. The Tao teaches that the universe is balanced and whole, following its own order, not our desires. If we acknowledge that order, and allow it to inform our thoughts, feelings, and actions, conflict disappears.

> *The Tao gives birth to all beings,*
> *nourishes them, maintains them,*
> *cares for them, comforts them, protects them, takes them back to itself,*

creating without possessing, acting without expecting,
   guiding without interfering.
That is why the love of the Tao
is in the very nature of things.

"So what do I do? Just 'go with the flow' not knowing where it leads? How 'New Age.' And besides, Sausalito's not in my territory."

"Perhaps what's troubling you is the sense of things as opposites and the belief that you have to choose between them. Is a river passive or active? If you say 'passive,' watch it erode rock and crumble houses. If you say 'active,' watch it effortlessly find the easy way to the sea. Imagine that you lived each day with as much simplicity of action, patience, and compassion as possible. Imagine that in every dealing with a customer, supplier, manager, or colleague, you tried to create as much real value as possible, and let the results work themselves out in time. Could you do better than that by trying to control things and people?"

Simplicity, Patience, Compassion

I have just three things to teach:
simplicity, patience, compassion.
These are your three greatest treasures.
Simple in actions and thoughts,
you return to the source of your being.
Patient with both friends and enemies,
you accord with the way things are.
Compassionate towards yourself,
you reconcile all beings in the world.

I have described my experience with the Tao as a journey, and am offering this book as a way for you to begin your own exploration and discovery. Simplicity allows you to trust yourself more deeply as you move into unfamiliar territory. Since you won't always know where you are, technique and control will be less helpful anyway. Try trusting your ability to be aware and to act powerfully and completely in each moment. Patience allows you to stop worrying so much about the future.

Since you can't know where you're going because the end doesn't exist yet, maps and plans aren't much help either. If you are compassionate towards yourself, you can work through the ebb and flow of events (what we call "success and failure"), learning as you go. If you're compassionate with customers, they'll make the journey with you.

Simplicity, patience, and compassion balance one another and resolve apparent conflicts within themselves. They work in synergy and their power is that of discovery, two qualities you and your customers will need to develop in each other, together.

> *The Master does his job*
> *and then stops.*
> *He understands that the universe*
> *is forever out of control,*
> *and that trying to dominate events*
> *goes against the current of the Tao.*
> *Because he believes in himself,*
> *he doesn't try to convince others.*
> *Because he is content with himself,*
> *he doesn't need others' approval.*
> *Because he accepts himself,*
> *the whole world accepts him.*

The standard arrangement of the *Tao Te Ching* contains 81 chapters. No one knows for sure how the 81 chapters were originally written and organized, or, for that matter, who wrote them. Lao Tzu may have been a historical person, or several people, or simply a generic name given to the wise sages of the period in which Taoism flourished, from around 500 to 250 B.C. Other scholars date the roots of Taoism and the *Tao Te Ching* as far back as 1800 B.C. The name "Lao Tzu" is actually not so much a name as a title or description, like "Wise Old Man," or "Old Geezer." I like the idea of "Old Geezer." It works well with the text of the *Tao Te Ching.*

As to the translations, every reader has his or her preferences. These are mine. The very first edition I read, by Gia-Fu Feng and Jane English, and published by Random House, still charms and surprises, like a mountain pool discovered at the turn of a trail. It is really two "translations," one in graceful language, the other in haunting, beautiful photographs that stimulate their own form of thought and meditation. Stephen Mitchell's translation, published by Harper Perennial Books, is more "modern" and immediately accessible to someone with no prior knowledge of the Tao. It "holds" the ancient thought in today's language without grasping, and flows like "melting ice," as the reviewer from the *New Republic* described it. I find myself continually returning to Mitchell's translation for its humor, clarity, and largeness of spirit. The translation by Man-Ho Kwok, Martin Palmer, and Jack Ramsay is deliberately, delightfully poetic, combining calligraphy, English text, and ancient Chinese art into a seamless whole.

Some scholars and translators begin the *Tao Te Ching* with the "Tao" section, Chapters 1-37, followed by the "Te" section, chapters 38-81. Others reverse that order. Martin Palmer suggests that the "original" *Tao Te Ching* consisted of 70 chapters, with the remaining 11 written at a later date than the original.

At the top of the stairs in my home I have placed pictures of my parents, along with other members of my family, so that I see them easily when I start each day, and see them again when I go to bed. My mother and father, both of whom are now gone, look out from their photographs with quiet smiles in their eyes. One needs to look carefully, because my father's face looks a little serious and my mother's a little shy. Twice a day, I step inside the photographs for a quiet moment or two, and look out through their eyes at their life together. Then I start and end the day with that same smile inside me, and I remember to be a little less serious and a little less shy, as they would have wanted.

Finding Without Looking

1 . No Way

If you're looking for the "right way" to achieve success, happiness, financial security, and approval from others, you won't find it. It doesn't exist.

If you stop looking, you notice it's always been there, plain to the eye and easy to follow.

Nobody can tell you where or what that way is; but it can be discovered and learned. No one else can tell you where that way will lead; but you can travel it safely. It is unique to each person, incapable of being duplicated or copied, and also timelessly universal.

The way of Tao is both simple and challenging because it asks us to let go of our fears and preconceptions, to release the pull of the things of this world as a driving force in our lives, and to become fully attentive to the spirit within us and all creation.

———————

WHAT'S THE "RIGHT WAY" TO SELL? Why are books and tapes that promise "The Answer" to making money and successful selling so popular?

Could it be our lack of trust in our own ability to discover the truth within ourselves, others, and the world?

If happiness is somewhere outside of us, then we are doomed to spend our lives chasing after it. That's a difficult search. Often when we get what we thought would make us happy, we discover we're still unsatisfied.

All of us know people who have been disappointed so often in this search that they give up looking, and resign themselves to unhappiness. If they feel angry at being disappointed, they make others unhappy.

What would it be like if, in reality, happiness were inside all of us: deep, strong, whole? All we would need to do then is learn to stop racing around, become more quiet and attentive, and discover what is already there.

Suppose we helped our customers reach the same discovery?

德 *What "way" have you followed over the past six months? Harried or peaceful? Purposeful or frantic? Loving or anxious? Answer the question for yourself, share your response with a friend, and listen to the feedback.*

2 . GOOD AND BAD

We seek for answers outside ourselves in someone else's "truth" because the world can often appear frighteningly confusing. In the face of that confusion, it often seems easier to divide things up into "Good" and "Bad." "Good" represents what we desire, "Bad" those things which seem to oppose our desires. But look again. Does not what we call "Good" contain "Bad"? What we call "Bad" also contain "Good"?

The more we struggle to achieve success because we think it represents "Good," the harder we have to fight to keep what we've gained at such cost against the efforts of "Bad" people.

Behind our often frantic efforts lurks our self-doubt.

"People must like and approve me."
"I must make more money to be successful."
"I must make others give me what I need."
"I must gain more status to feel valued."
"If I do not control people they will control me."

The harder we try to overcome those fears, the more likely our efforts will produce the opposite result. Try as we may, we never get quite enough approval, or money, or status. Yet we can't deny the existence of these fears; they are part of us. If we attack them, we wound ourselves. So we are caught:

The more we talk, the less people listen.
The more we get, the more we seem to need.
The more we demand, the less people give willingly.
The more we try to control the future, or dwell on the past, the less meaning we experience in each day.

————

WHEN WE APPLY THE LABELS "Good" and "Bad" to others or ourselves, we blind ourselves to the possibilities constantly present in people and situations. What makes you "Good" as a salesperson? The fact that you succeed in earning money? When times are tough and success harder to achieve, does that make you "Bad"? It is the same with customers. Sometimes our "Bad" customers are our best teachers. Sometimes focusing only on our "Good" customers makes us lazy and inattentive.

德 *Take a moment and ask yourself: "What about the way I relate to people do I like the most?" Then call one of your "best" customers, and say (in your own words): "You know, I've been thinking about how I relate to people in business. What's it like for you to work with me?" Listen to the response and compare it with your self-assessment.*

3

3. PRAISE AND REWARDS

*If you habitually react or respond to circumstances, where does the power
lie in these situations? It clearly lies outside you, in the circumstances.
Therefore, because the power does not reside in you, you are powerless and
the circumstances are all-powerful.*

ROBERT FRITZ

Seek riches, fame, approval, or public acclaim, and you pour water
into a bottomless hole. The more you pour in, the wider the hole
becomes.

If we seek praise and rewards to make ourselves feel valued, then all
our value is tied up in those things and not strongly alive within
us. Remove the praise and we are empty. Deny the reward and we
are poor. It is the same for others. Praise someone's work and you
encourage their dependency on praise and feed the need for more.

––––––––––

ONE REASON, AS SALESPEOPLE, we seek praise and rewards is that we live so
much of our work life in an atmosphere of resistance and rejection. "I'm busy. Call
me in six months." "We're not interested." "We use somebody else." "I already
have what I want." "Go away." The external praise we receive that says "You're
O.K." is comforting. The rewards appear to nourish our self-esteem.

Look again.

The key is the hunger, the need to be approved in order to feel successful.
Hunger makes us do stupid things and weakens our resolve. The need for praise
hurts us in other ways. If we doubt our own worth, then the praise of others
means nothing. "I'm really not that good." No amount of praise or rewards fills
that void or heals that hurt.

德 *Write down the rewards you work for. What goals drive your
daily actions? Are they internal? External? A mixture? Do
they match what you believe are your values?*

*Ask yourself, "If I received all the external rewards and praise I
seek, would I then be happy and fulfilled?" Ask yourself, "What inner
values might be more nourishing?"*

4. LOOKING INSIDE

What we call "Tao," or "God," or "spirituality," or "truth" cannot be captured in language, felt with the senses, or contained in the mind. Yet it is inside us and all things. That paradox can make us uneasy because of our desire to describe, feel, and know the truth.

Truth is, before the world first was. It creates, but was not created. It is a spring that never dries up, flowing from a source none of us can imagine. We can drink from it and be nourished.

Release the words and the meaning will appear.

Stop looking and your vision will clear.

Unclench the fist and you will be touched.

Be silent and you will hear.

————

IT TAKES COURAGE TO MEET each day as a salesperson, allowing things to unfold truthfully rather than trying to make them happen according to our desires. But if we observe salespeople who are truly "successful," we can see their commitment to trust living within them. It lives, as well, in their daily dealings with their customers. We probably feel it in our own relationships with them. They have made a choice; each of us can do the same. That choice begins when we confront our fears: being "alone," not meeting others' expectations, not being respected, valued, or needed by others. In the very act of examining those fears we stand apart from them.

If we feel nervous, anxious, stressed, or angry, we are creating those feelings inside ourselves by our own thoughts and actions. We can choose to do otherwise. The gift of being a salesperson is that we have the opportunity to make that choice every day, each time we are face-to-face with a customer.

德 *Imagine that you are able to have a conversation with yourself. Ask yourself how you are feeling during a typical work day. Balanced? Focused? Relaxed? Happy? Purposeful? Or the opposite?*

What might it be like if you met the same challenges that now create anxiety in your life with calm attentiveness and trustworthy actions?

Name your greatest fear or stress inducer and share it with a colleague. "I'm often afraid that...." Pay attention to how you feel and what you hear.

5

5. SUPERIOR AND INFERIOR

None of us chose to be born into this world. Few of us choose when and in what way we will leave it. From that fundamental insecurity arises pride: our desire to feel "special," to believe that we are important. From that fundamental insecurity arises despair: the feeling that we are valueless and unimportant. Pride comforts us in the belief that we are, at least, better than other people. Pride's mirror, despair, is the fear that we are not.

Is it possible that both pride and despair are ways of denying the existence of God's grace?

Just because God is not a thing does not mean that God is nothing.
A little humility is in order.

JOHN HEIDER

———

MANY OF US WERE TAUGHT, as children, that to be "good" meant being "better" than someone else. That lesson was learned in competitive play with our friends, in quarrels with our siblings, and was reinforced by an educational system that often valued the grade or test score more than the learning.

Generations of salespeople took this lesson to heart: "success" meant climbing over, past, or on top of others, in the desire to be "better." "Failure" meant losing that race. But now, the "ladder of success" we were taught to climb leans precariously against a collapsing building—or runs in a circle like a squirrel in a cage. Managers learned the same lesson, seeking not personal power but power over other people, only to find their power was able to accomplish very little of real significance.

Which is really better: to be "superior" to another person or to be wholly good within ourselves?

Therefore, insisting on being "better" than another person degrades ourselves and them.

德 *List five people you feel "superior" to. Spend the next few days identifying strength or value in those people which your pride may have caused you to overlook. Take the time to directly let them know what it is about them you value. Do it before this week is over.*

Do the same with five people you feel "inferior" to. Spend the next few days discovering ways you can create real value in your dealings with them. Act on these opportunities before this week is over.

6

6. POWER

Why try to seize power from others or use power against them when, by being quiet and receptive, we can find it within ourselves, inexhaustible, patiently waiting for us to awaken to its presence?

MUCH OF THE TRAINING many of us received as salespeople turns out to be untrustworthy, because it centers on what we must do to people. Because we are taught that success results from aggressiveness, we turn our customers and colleagues into enemies to conquer.

Selling, when we think of it as a struggle, is a struggle. Consider the techniques we learn:

- Getting past the secretary
- Getting in the door
- Getting the customer's attention
- Making the customer listen
- Uncovering needs
- Trying to "educate" the customer
- Defeating real objections
- Smoking out "hidden" concerns
- Combating indifference and rejection
- Overcoming price pressure
- Closing the sale—making the customer say "yes"

Observe productive, happy salespeople at work. They don't appear to struggle at all. They are partners with their customers. They share a common goal: maximizing the customer's success through the salesperson's products or services. Their dynamic is not "me against you" but "you and me against the challenge." The power both enjoy is the power both create together.

Think of selling situations in which you feel the need to be powerful. Examine where that power comes from. Yourself alone, or you and the customer? In each case, ask yourself what would happen if you shared the power to achieve success with the customer. Suppose you defined success not as what you did, alone, but what you both accomplished together? How would that impact your technique? How might it impact the results?

德 *For the next week, step away from situations in which you feel the urge to take charge. Do as little as possible and notice what happens. Share how you feel about all this with a friend or trusted colleague. If you want to be really bold, share how you feel with the customer you've just "empowered."*

7

The earth has existed and will endure long after we have disappeared into dust. It is a gift that was not made by people but rather created for all living things to enjoy wisely.

To enjoy what you most deeply desire, care about the well-being of other people and the world around you as much as you value your own happiness.

————

BURTON HALL TELLS THE STORY of answering an ad for a five-room steam-cleaning package offered by a major department chain. A woman with a strong voice and pleasant manner answered the phone. When he described the job he needed done in his office, she immediately pointed out that the service they were offering through the ad was not really "steam cleaning," as the phrase suggests, but rather more of a strong surface vacuuming.

"So what we have here," Burton remarked with some irritation, "is a classic 'bait and switch.' You advertise one thing and provide something else!" "I'm afraid so," the woman answered without hesitation. "I'm sorry, but that's what it's about. I don't believe in misleading customers." Her honesty was startling, even refreshing.

"Tell me what you really need," she said, "and I'll tell you what it will really cost, so you can figure out if it's worthwhile getting it done."

"Normally I'd never deal with a company that used such tactics," Burton adds. "But her blunt honesty and forthright manner more than made up for what was a cheap marketing ploy. Instead of a 'slam dunk' rejection, she got an order, and I got what I needed done, at an acceptable price. Talk about a *Miracle on 34th Street!* She had more integrity than her company. Come to think of it, maybe the spirit of 'you can get it at Gimbels' isn't completely dead."

Truthful selling embraces a paradox. If we really take care of our customers, they find ways of taking care of us. The greater the quality of our caring, the stronger their response.

One way to achieve balance within this paradox is to stop wanting things from our customers; for example, a sale. When our customers stop being "things" we seek to manipulate within the limits of our world, they begin to become real people in the world we both inhabit. The freedom from needing the customer to do something for us allows us to act caringly toward them.

德 *Before each sales call or client meeting this week, ask yourself, "What's the greatest gift I could give this person right now?" Give that gift without telling anybody what you're doing.*

Practicing:
FINDING WITHOUT LOOKING

1. **Start breathing**
    Real people breathe from their heels; ordinary people breathe from their throats.
    CHUANG-TZU

"I want to inspire my customers," a salesperson once told me. She had forgotten that inspire means to "breathe in." We can't inspire our customers unless we inspire ourselves first. Right now, as you read this, allow your breathing to deepen until you can feel the breath rising up from the soles of your feet through your entire body. Continue breathing deeply and fully as you let your body relax. As you exhale, consciously release whatever tense or anxious thoughts you may have. Give yourself this moment of peacefulness. Before and during each sales call, repeat this exercise, so you can give the same gift of peacefulness to your customers.

2. **Open your mind**
    The quest for certainty is an invitation to defeat.
    JOHN DEWEY

While we may not actually come out and say "I want to control my customers," the desire to control our destiny and create a "safe" future may cause us to do just that. Certainly all conventional sales techniques are rooted in the desire to control customer behavior and manipulate a buying decision. The desire to control may give us the illusion of safety; it also robs us of the chance to create real value with each customer, spontaneously and authentically. "Opening your mind" means letting go of the desire to control things and trusting that if we do our best work, day by day, we will be fulfilled over time.

3. **Open your ears**
    Seek first to understand, then to be understood.
    SAINT AUGUSTINE

The desire to control outcomes causes us to hear what we expect to hear, and block out all the rest—especially if what the other person is saying doesn't match our needs. If we are anxious, fearful, or trying to control things, it's easy for us to distort messages by unconsciously filtering them through our emotions. We believe a customer is angry at us, displeased about something, may not trust us, or is trying to get rid of us. In fact, the customer may be asking a simple, "unloaded" question. Our emotions cause us to turn that simple statement into something else—a threat or a challenge. "Opening your ears" means hearing what the customer says, with no assumptions. It means working patiently to understand their world as they describe it, without expectation or judgment.

4. **Open your eyes**

What you see is what you get. Stop looking, start seeing.

If all you notice when you look at the outer world is what is "bad," "ugly," "disappointing," "wrong," or "hopeless," before long those things become the landscape of your inner world. Pretty soon you'll feel the need to confirm your belief that the world is a harsh, pressured, hopeless place, so the only things you'll notice are the distressful things you're looking for. "Stop looking, start seeing" means allowing yourself to see, in the present moment, the goodness within you and others—in all its beauty and strength. Once you understand that, you are free to see the potential goodness in any situation you encounter and any customer you work with. Celebrate that goodness as the first thing upon waking; make it the last thing you do before retiring—instead of assaulting your spirit with the TV "news."

5. **Open your heart**

"Us against the problem," not "me against you."

Instead of manipulating customers to buy what you sell, work with them collaboratively so they are able to buy what they need. "Opening your heart" means finding ways to create genuine partnership with customers; it changes the dynamic of the sales call from a self-focused, "one-night stand" to something stronger and long-lasting, like a deep friendship, a sharing, mutually-supportive marriage, or a loving relationship. Not all customers, of course, will choose to enter into that kind of partnership with you; the ones who do will help you succeed.

6. **Open your spirit**

We are responsible for our own effectiveness, for our own happiness, and ultimately, I would say, for most of our circumstances.
STEPHEN COVEY

We get the world we choose to live in. You can choose to live in a world of scarcity and fear, or choose to live in a world of abundance and love. If you choose scarcity and fear, acknowledge the consequences of that choice. If you choose abundance and love, acknowledge the consequences of that choice. Living by choice in a world of decisions and consequences restores to us the freedom that the pressures of today's world appear to have taken away. Offer the same choice to your customers.

7. **Open your life: Be the kind of salesperson you would buy from**

What you do is who you are.

List the actions other salespeople do to you as a customer that drive you crazy, make you angry, or suspicious. Use those as a check on your own sales behaviors. Let your actions reflect your beliefs and most important values.

Powerless Power

When practical people hear about the Tao they laugh at it.
If they didn't laugh, it wouldn't be the Tao.

For American business professionals, the Tao represents an extraordinary contradiction of everything we've been taught and all the messages our world appears to be sending. At a time when there is enormous pressure to "work harder, longer, faster, smarter, get more results, make more sales, beat the competition," the Tao says "Simplify. Don't try so hard. Take it easy."

Do without doing.
Achieve without effort.

The message comes at a time when there is widespread fear of the future. "Will I have a job?" "Will I be able to take care of my family's future?" "Can I even provide for my own?" "How can I trust the people in charge? All they care about is themselves." "What kind of world am I leaving to my children?" And the Tao says, "Take care of today. The future will happen however it happens."

Live each day completely. Sleep in peace.
Greet the new day with joy. You are already eternal in spirit.

At a time in which "take care of Number One" has become the mantra of survival, the Tao tells us to act selflessly against our "best interests" and innate sense of caution. "Once you accept the reality of change, there's nothing left to fear."

In a business culture which is still aggressively "male," in spite of the patient efforts of women to shatter the glass ceiling, and in which the dominant business culture is still a military model, the Tao says, "Know the male. Practice the female."

So the Tao simply cannot be approached through "reason," "logic," and "practicality." It doesn't make sense on those terms. But if we look thoughtfully, the world we live in makes increasingly less sense on its own terms, day by day. The stock market booms while spendable income for most families continues to drop below 1970 levels. Our cities are becoming uninhabitable and we lack the strength of will and resources to halt the downward slide. Regardless of how well we've insulated ourselves from the consequences of the society we have created, the hard facts tell the truth: we are destroying the planet's ability to sustain all life (including our own) at a frighteningly accelerating rate.

The Tao is a 2,500-year-old way to restore the wholeness we are searching for.

8. EFFORTLESSNESS

Truth, like water, flows through, under, and over the created world, bringing life, nourishing, cleansing, replenishing itself in a timeless cycle. Truth does not exist solely for people, and thus we call it destructive when it harms the things we create and covet. Seeking to control and use water, we wind up polluting it and wasting it.

Without water we would quickly perish; but if all human life were to disappear, the waves would still surge across the ocean's depth, rivers would follow their wise journey to the sea, and the life-bringing rain would still fall.

The water's wisdom: "I do not blame the rock for being solid and immobile. Nor do I regret being fluid and supple."

> *In dwelling, be close to the land.*
> *In meditation, go deep in the heart.*
> *In dealing with others, be gentle and kind.*
> *In speech, be true.*
> *In ruling, be just.*
> *In business, be competent.*
> *In action, watch the timing.*

GIA-FU FENG AND JANE ENGLISH

THE WISE SALESPERSON ADAPTS easily and effortlessly to situations and people. The truthful salesperson seeks to create real value without worrying about the immediacy of reward. First the action, then the reward, in its own time. Action follows the path of least resistance, bringing clarity to problems and life to people, flowing effortlessly around obstacles, seeking the easy, common-sense response to an opportunity or solution to a problem.

德 *Suppose, as a salesperson, you were able to stop thinking about the results you wanted and worrying about the response of others. What if you allowed yourself to act naturally and spontaneously with customers to create as much value in the sales relationship as possible?*

How would that change how you think? How you feel? How you and the customer act together?

"Enough is as good as a feast."

- If you fill a cup to the brim, you can't carry it without spilling.

- The wise gardener always lets some plants remain unharvested so there is seed for the coming year.

- The skilled warrior never over-sharpens the sword's blade nor the skilled carpenter the tool's edge.

- The skilled speaker knows that silence is more powerful than speech. Only in silence can the speaker's words enter the listener's mind to nourish thoughts and inspire action.

———————

THE ADVICE IS EASIER TO SAY than do: Know when to stop persuading and let the customer buy. Know when to stop talking and listen. Know when to stop selling and walk away.

It is better to keep your mouth shut and have people wonder if you're a fool, than open it and remove all doubt.

We can't learn these lessons from books, manuals, tapes, or other people. They are not contained in anyone else's "Surefire Secrets of Selling" or "Ten Steps to Instant Success." Happily, we can learn to find the answers in ourselves.

Notice cause and effect. If you pursue money and security, notice how people become jealous or envious in the presence of your desire. If you make a big deal about your expertise, notice how others push back, or become suddenly stupid. If you want approval from others, notice how hard it is to get and how little pleasure getting it brings you.

Try to push against the customer a little less, and observe if the customer enters the space you have just created. Often that is as easy as responding to your inner urgency by saying nothing at all.

Notice when customers create room themselves, and then enter that space yourself, as a friend. Often that is as easy as listening deeply to what they say and supporting their idea where they want to take it instead of insisting on your own direction.

德 *Each day, practice silence, in increasingly longer intervals (you may need to start with a few seconds). Leave an idea unfinished and wait for the customer to finish the thought. Record what silence feels like in a daily journal.*

10. SHARING POWER

Knowing the truth, can you let others find it for themselves?

In the presence of great opportunity, can you remain calm and flexible?

In the presence of your own fears can you remain relaxed and focused?

In the presence of others' fears can you remain balanced and strong?

Having power, can you share it rather than wield it?

Can you walk among warring parties and mediate without taking sides?

When confronted by problems, can you let the solution arise on its own?

Can you open the door of wisdom and then stand back to let others enter on their own?

––––––––––

AS SALESPEOPLE, MANAGERS, executives, and consultants, we are challenged and rewarded for being "problem solvers." We believe our value to our organization or our customers is based on our ability to fix things and create solutions. "Here it is. I have the answer. Listen to me."

When we are able to do something that blocks or defeats others, this sense of ourselves as problem solvers is appealing—even seductive—because we feel powerful and in control.

Consider what else comes along with this satisfying feeling of power:
- Impatience with others' solutions and suggestions.
- Blindness to the weaknesses in our own thinking.
- The need to find, even force a solution.
- Greater difficulty in letting go of our ideas if they don't work as we expected.

As salespeople, all the power we gather to ourselves we take away from the customer. When it comes time for the customer to help us, he or she is powerless to do so. Our real purpose as salespeople must be to create positive energy and power for the customer to use, not to take power away from the customer and ourselves. That power we share comes from the calm center within us, not the frantic, pressured world outside.
- Hold without grasping.
- Create in order to release.
- Save your best work for the moments you are unobserved.
- Lead without commanding.

 Have a conversation today with someone you have a power conflict with. Find a way to share power with that person.

The wheel's center must be empty to receive the axle.

A vase must be empty to hold flowers.

A room is a useless space until the builder cuts holes in the walls: windows to see through and doors for passage.

The real value in things is not apparent at the surface but lies, rather, within the quiet, empty center.

————

The Master Nan-in had a visitor who came to inquire about Zen. But instead of listening, the visitor kept talking about his own ideas.

After a while, Nan-in served tea. He poured tea into his visitor's cup until it was full, then he kept on pouring, until the tea spilled over the rim of the cup and onto the floor.

Finally the visitor could not restrain himself. "Don't you see it's full?" he said. "You can't get any more in!"

"Just so," replied Nan-in, stopping at last. "And like this cup, you are filled with your own ideas. How can you expect me to give you Zen unless you offer me an empty cup?"

IT IS SAID THAT THE WORDS we utter and hear are only a fraction of the messages we send and receive in turn. When we focus only on what we and others say, we may grasp the words but miss the meaning.

Sometimes as salespeople, we barely hear the customer's words because we're so busy in our own minds trying to figure out what we want to say next, in response to a message we may have completely misunderstood.

Yet we know that our best opportunities for success come when we are fully, completely aware of what is happening within and around us in the sales call. This awareness comes with emptiness.

Anxiety and urgency make this kind of "empty," fully receptive listening and observation difficult. Our brain fills with a thousand clamoring thoughts. "What if they ask a question I can't answer?" "What if I get an objection I can't counter?" "What if I can't think of the proper arguments to change how they think?" "How do I know they're telling the truth?" "What benefits do they really want to hear?" "What are they really willing to pay? How do I keep from overpricing the deal?"

德 *The next time you're in a conversation with a colleague, boss, or customer and feel anxiety start to intrude, focus all your attention on what you're really hearing from the other person. Breathe. Empty your mind; open your spirit.*

12. INSIGHT

We dance around a ring and suppose.
The secret sits in the center, and knows.

ROBERT FROST

We live in a deafening, blinding world, sounds jostling and crowding the thoughts in our mind, a thousand conflicting images blurring our vision. Seeking knowledge, we drown instead in a flood of information. Desiring insight, we are confounded by too many choices.

———

INSIGHT COMES FROM THE INSIDE, not the outside. If we allow time for quietness, we create opportunities for listening deeply to ourselves. Our body knows when we're "doing things right." Tension, uneasiness, sickness, pain. These are our body's ways of saying we need to grow, change, and become whole again. Joy, peacefulness, calmness, hope. This is how our body tells us we are acting appropriately and effectively. Our inner self can speak to us if we let ourselves listen.

It is the same with our clients. Instead of worrying about what they think or mean, notice the messages their body is sending them.

If they are joyful or hopeful, share in their well-being; celebrate it. If they are troubled, seek to help them become whole.

Learn to trust the physical messages more than the words.

If you don't know what a client means or intends, ask, don't guess.

德 *We can increase our awareness. Practice observing silence, hearing inaction, and touching emptiness. In a crowd of people, ignore the words and let yourself "listen" to the actions with your eyes. When listening, notice what is not being said. Pay attention to what people are not doing.*

Look for moments when you can observe others closely without your attention being obvious. Notice the changes of color in their skin around their face and neck. Notice the level and changes of tension in their shoulders, forehead, and lower lip.

As you observe others in a quiet, respectful way, practice matching your breathing to another person's rhythm. Empty your mind of conscious thoughts and just allow yourself to get in harmony with that person for a little while. In sales calls, apply the same relaxed attentiveness with clients.

17

13. FAILURE AND DISGRACE

Success is the father of failure; the more success we get, the more we worry about losing it. The more we worry about failure, the less open we are to success.

───────

THE FEAR OF FAILURE AND DISGRACE is a powerful motivator. Having our plans, hopes, and desires frustrated or blocked can feel like dying, so powerful is the blow to our self. Some people, to protect themselves from this "little death of the self," unconsciously lower their goals and expect less from themselves so they won't be so disappointed with "failure."

"Well, I didn't really want it all that badly." "It's not that important." "I really couldn't have done it anyway." "You just can't deal with those people. It's impossible."

Sometimes that protection takes the form of victimization. "It's not really my fault. My hands were tied." "My boss messed everything up." "The company wouldn't have let me do it anyway."

Others inflate their sense of well-being and accomplishment to convince themselves that they're doing O.K. "My customers all love me." (I don't have customers who don't love me.)

When pushed, people who work hard to prolong their fantasy of well-being can easily become angry or violent in defense of that fantasy. "What do you mean I made a mistake!" "What a stupid analysis. Anybody can see that the numbers are still good!" "You're wrong! I'm right!"

What a sad predicament to be in: if we run from the possibility of failure, we destroy all the sources of happiness outside us as well as our inner power to respond. If we seek to insulate ourselves from the natural misfortune of the world, we wind up closing ourselves within the cocoon of our fantasies. (But no butterfly escapes from that cocoon.)

"Disgrace" and "failure" become less punishing when we recognize our own relative unimportance and let go of the hold of others' opinions on our peace of mind. To whom does it really matter that we achieve momentary fame? Lavish praise is often how other people make themselves feel worthwhile. It is the same with others' criticism and blame. They often criticize and blame us out of their own feelings of worthlessness and fear. If we acknowledge the power of their fear over them, we give it power over our own lives as well.

 Find ways to reward people—clients or colleagues—who freely admit their own failures or mishaps.

The harder we look for insight into the significance of things, the less we see.

The more we strain to listen to the words, the less we hear.

The tighter we grasp, the less we hold.

Nevertheless, what can't easily be seen, heard, or touched truthfully exists.

The more we try to reason from the past in order to control the present, the less meaning we find in the changing future. Who can follow the river's course once it enters the sea?

The more anxiety we develop about the future, the less happiness we experience in the present and the less comfort we find in the past. Who can predict where next year's rain will fall?

————

IT IS IMPORTANT TO UNDERSTAND that what we perceive through our senses is filtered through our hopes and fears before it reaches our minds. What we expect to find, whether good or bad, we usually discover. What we fear to see often appears as if summoned. The meaning we take from others' actions and words is the meaning we anticipated. "See, I told you so." "I knew it would happen that way."

Underneath and beyond the meanings we create about people and events, life is unfolding.

We see it more easily with the inner eye of calm reflection than by hard staring. Parts of a picture that our intent vision blurs, or obscures, or simply misses, become apparent when we relax and allow the picture to come to us.

We hear more clearly by listening quietly not only to the words, but to all the actions that happen around those words, to what is not being said, and especially to ourselves as we interact with those messages. The meaning is there. It's just "spoken" in a soft voice.

When we stop trying to seize things, we open ourselves for things to come to us.

When we live fully in the present, the lessons of the past retain all their value and lose their ability to hurt us.

When we live fully in the present, the future becomes less frightening: a realization of one positive, productive day flowing into the next.

德 *Write down your expectations for every major problem or opportunity this week. In as many of these situations as possible, try to act with greater openness, spontaneity, and awareness of what's happening moment by moment. Spend as much time as possible in the "here and now." At the end of the week, notice what's happened.*

Practicing:
POWERLESS POWER

1.   **Start with a question, not a speech**

Many salespeople kill any chance of a good relationship with customers (and a profitable sale) by launching into a product demonstration or a "pitch" as soon as they sit down with the customer. Think about what message that action sends to customers:

"I don't care about your needs, just my products." "I'm not interested in you, only in me." "I'm going to try to sell you something whether you need it or not." "I'm no different from any of the other salespeople who call on you."

Instead of presenting five benefits, state one, simply, then pause and allow the customer to think about it. Notice the customer's reaction, and follow up with a question that invites the customer to pursue his or her own thoughts about what you've said.

"Our {products/services} help customers {state a real benefit to your customers}. What kinds of challenges are you facing?"

2.   **Don't pick up a hot potato**

Customers have been trained to listen (barely) to a sales pitch. Some customers, therefore, appear to want to hear your "pitch" and may even demand it. "O.K. I'll give you two minutes. What new products are you offering?" "You're the expert; tell me what I should be buying." "Run me through how this thing works in detail." If you want to create value for yourself and your customers, resist the invitation to start talking. Prepare one to two-sentence statements about how your products and services have helped customers solve problems and capitalize on opportunities, then ask the customer or prospect what comparable problems or opportunities they're dealing with.

3.   **Use the customers' language in your own speech**

Listen to your customers, and note the language they use—their specific words—as they talk about problems and opportunities. Instead of paraphrasing in your language (or ignoring their ideas completely), use their language.

A simple way to develop this skill is to listen to others' conversation in a social or non-sales situation. What are the words they use to express ideas that are important to them? Practice briefly restating their ideas using their words. As you practice this, you will notice how little people really listen to each other. Make the commitment to become the best listener your customers know.

4.   **Help customers think for themselves**

When you hear words that you believe are important concepts, ideas, concerns, or values to the customer, invite the customer to explore the meaning of those ideas. A simple way to do that is to ask "What about {that idea} is important to you?" Practice asking that question within the first three minutes of every sales call and listening to the answer.

5. Listen and question in depth—listen and look before you leap

Instead of leaping on what you believe is a sales opportunity, learn more. When you think you have identified an opportunity, discipline yourself to probe and confirm it with at least three additional questions. Simple, useful follow-up questions are:

- "Could you tell me more about that?"
- "What would be a specific example?"
- "What would getting that [accomplishing that] mean to you?"
- "Suppose you weren't able to [accomplish that]? What would that mean?"

6. Make ideas tangible

Customers speak in generalities; they think and dream in specific images. When you speak in concrete, specific examples you help customers imagine what they mean by what they say. Ask questions that help customers talk about what they are seeing, hearing, and feeling. As you listen to these specific images, try to record them in your mind as pictures, sounds, or feelings.

7. Stop fighting your customers

The easiest place to start is in normal conversation. Every time you interrupt, try to correct the customer, or push your own ideas, you are making things needlessly harder on yourself. How to change? You can start by completely removing "Yes, BUT…" from your vocabulary. An old sales buddy of mine put it succinctly. "When we say 'Yes, BUT…' customers know that everything before the 'BUT' was bullshit."

Instead, simply substitute "Yes, AND…" for "Yes, BUT…" and notice the response you get in return.

One of the best-loved Zen stories tells of the two monks on a journey who stopped by a ford across a swollen river. Standing helplessly by the river's edge, unable to cross, was a very pretty young woman. One monk, without thinking, picked her up and carried her across. The monks continued their journey, and after several hours of walking in silence, the other monk exploded. "How could you have carried a woman like that in your arms!" "Oh," his partner replied, "I put her down hours ago. Why are you still carrying her?"

THE "ART" OF THE TAO is in letting things happen rather than trying to make them happen. What separates this "letting things happen" from mere helpless passivity or indifference is the complete harmony with something larger than ourselves, call it Tao, or faith. We allow ourselves to be moved by "it" rather than forcing our will on events.

Stephen Covey, in *The Seven Habits of Highly Effective People*, calls it the "clear center from which you consistently derive a high degree of security, guidance, wisdom, and power, empowering your productivity and giving congruency and harmony to every part of your life." His book is a helpful way for people to discover that center within themselves. Once discovered, the graceful action is to trust it and let it "use" you.

The challenge of allowing the center to be the source of our daily action is described in Eugen Herrigel's *Zen in the Art of Archery*.

> "Don't think of what you have to do, don't consider how to carry it out!" {the Master} exclaimed. "The shot will only go smoothly when it takes the archer himself by surprise. It must be as if the bowstring suddenly cut through the thumb that holds it. You mustn't open the right hand on purpose."

> "Do you know why you cannot wait for the shot and why you get out of breath before it has come? The right shot at the right moment does not come because you do not let go of yourself. You do not wait for fulfillment, but brace yourself for failure. So long as that is so, you have no choice but to call forth something yourself that ought to happen independently of you, and so long as you call it forth your hand will not open in the right way—like the hand of a child. Your hand does not burst open like the skin of a ripe fruit."

> "The right art," cried the Master, "is purposeless, aimless! The more obstinately you try to learn how to shoot the arrow for the sake of hitting the goal, the less you will succeed in the one and the further the other will recede. What stands in your way is that you have a much too willful will. You think that what you do not do yourself does not happen."

22

Becoming Centered

15. TRUST

Think of the wisest people you know, named and unnamed, in your culture or beliefs. Not seeking power over others, they brought power to all from a center we cannot fathom. We can only observe their actions.

Carefully, gracefully stepping across the swollen river's smooth stones, as untroubled within the turmoil as on the farther, peaceful shore.

Entering a dangerous place alertly, poised, embracing the darkness, unafraid of the shadows or the sharp, sudden noise.

At ease with all people as if the stranger were a close friend.

Relaxed, like water letting go its frozen grip to thaw back again into stream. As simple as the block of wood which already contains the sculptor's future statue. As full of presence as an empty cave, as clear as a deep pool.

The archer, competing for an insignificant clay vessel, shot with great expertise: effortlessly, gracefully, accurately. When the prize was increased to a bronze ornament, his hands started trembling, and only with the greatest effort could he still hit the target. When the prize was increased to gold, his eyes failed him. Squinting as if he were going blind, shaking like a windblown leaf, he missed the target completely, and the laughter of the crowd only increased his shame. His skills had not deteriorated, only his trust in them, as he allowed the imagined value of the prize to deaden his nerves and cloud his vision.

AT THE CENTER OF OUR IMPATIENCE is a lack of trust in ourselves, the customer, and the process we create together. This lack of trust traps both of us, destroying our freedom to create.

We doubt our ability to be strong, or we fear rejection, so we make concessions and promises that hurt us. We doubt the value of our compassion, or fear being "used," and so withhold our support and concern.

How does one act wisely as a salesperson? Waiting patiently for the moment to act, knowing that it will come. Quiet amidst the noise, clear in the silence. Strong and forceful in the moment without wasted energy, holding nothing back. Stopping when the work of that moment is done.

德 *Ask your best customers: "Who are the people you trust the most? Why do you trust them?" Use that definition of trust to measure your own value.*

16. No Desires

"Waiting patiently" means relaxing the hold of desires and fears in one's heart while the shifting, moving events of the world pass through turmoil back again into peaceful balance.

The juggler does not follow the spinning balls with her eyes. The balls merely float into relaxed, intuitive hands.

The actions of this world are like this. They spin around us. If we follow their movement with our eyes we easily become confused. Wait. Be ready.

When we wait patiently, it is easier to be tolerant.

If we are tolerant, we perceive more—without straining to see.

When we act with perception, it is easier to be patient.

> *Immersed in the wonder of the Tao,*
> *you can deal with whatever life brings you.*
> STEPHEN MITCHELL

―――――――

MANY SALESPEOPLE I TALK WITH describe themselves as being busy, busy, busy. I observe them impatiently scurrying after a future that runs faster than their most frenetic actions or seeking to escape an unfriendly and rapidly advancing past. "I have a thousand contacts. How can I possibly serve them all?" "I have too much to do already, and then they want me to fill out all these reports." "My customers want more from me than I can give. How can I satisfy all these needs?" "I'm running around here so fast my hair's on fire!"

It helps to remember that the things we really need are simple and few: air to breathe, food to eat, healthy exercise, shelter, restful sleep. Everything else consists of wants, not needs, which means we are free to choose what we want. We can choose desires that harm us or others, or choose not to desire those things. "I may feel I want this. Do I really need it?"

 Keep your desires simple: Before each client meeting repeat to yourself one of the following phrases. Notice what happens in the meeting.

> *"I want to say less and listen more."*
> *"I want to ask more questions and talk less."*
> *"I want to force less and discover more."*
> *"I want to act caringly and courageously in this meeting."*
> *"I want to bring clarity to this meeting for both of us."*

25

People follow popular leaders like sheep.

They flee harsh leaders like frightened birds.

They crouch under the feet of cruel leaders, waiting their own chance to bite.

With the best leaders, people say, "Look what we did ourselves."

Popular leaders use words like candy, offered to innocent children by a stranger.

Harsh leaders use words like a whip.

Cruel leaders use them like a knife.

The best leaders (teachers, parents, salespeople, managers) say little, and merely act.

———

TRUST YOUR CUSTOMERS to be able to discover the truth for themselves. It is within them as surely as it is within you. Assist the sales call in the positive way it is unfolding, rather than trying to make it conform to your desires.

If you must lead for awhile, be ready to step back, once the way is clear again, so the customer may proceed. Ask the customer for direction rather than pointing it out yourself. Throw light on the path, not brambles.

德 *Try creating opportunities for your customers to take the lead. One way to do that is to recognize your own urgency to solve the customer's problem or to "close the sale." That urgency often translates into pressure on the customer exactly when that pressure is most harmful: at the moment the customer is making the decision to buy.*

Step away from that urgency. Choose not to act on the self-generated pressure to take charge and force a close.

As clearly as possible, summarize the current situation, and the consequences facing the customer, then ask the customer how he or she wants to handle the situation. At the "close" of the sale, you need to be most open.

Since the customer may initially feel unwilling or unable to take that risk, be prepared to be patient. Continue asking questions that help the customer see both the issue and their own choices more clearly.

18. The Center of Things

Once you leave the path of simple consciousness, you enter the labyrinth of cleverness, competition, and imitation.

JOHN HEIDER

When we forget the truth at the center of things, preachers start teaching goodness, morality, and compassion.

When we forget the truth at the center of things, clever people arise to proclaim their wisdom (and others' stupidity).

When we forget the truth at the center of things, parents start talking about devotion to family and obedience.

When we forget the truth at the center of things, men and women, different races and cultures, all begin looking for leaders who will justify their own separate importance and the worthlessness of people who are different from themselves.

When we forget the truth at the center of things, patriots step forward and unsheathe the sword.

———

FOR SALESPEOPLE, "the truth at the center of things" is a simple choice: we are there either to help the customer, or to use the customer to get what we want. We can fool ourselves into believing that customers don't notice our intention only if we ignore our own experience as consumers and purchasers. We know when salespeople are trying to pressure us, or are ignoring our needs to satisfy their own. Why in the world should we imagine the people we sell to are any less aware?

If we allow ourselves to use our customers for our own gain, we naturally create resistance. That resistance becomes the source for all sorts of techniques designed to reduce the resistance our intention has caused in the first place. But since those techniques, themselves, are manipulative, they cause more resistance. Selling becomes tough.

So our managers start encouraging us to combat the resistance by setting quotas, punishing failure, and rewarding us when we successfully "make a sale." In time, those rewards can become the reason we sell.

Meanwhile, most of our customers continue to ask: "Understand my goals. If possible, help me see them more clearly than I do now. Value my concerns and respect my fears. They may not seem rational to you but they're my concerns and fears. Give me real choices and clear consequences so I can make a good buying decision. Promise what you can keep; keep what you promise. Be there when I need you. Help me."

德 *Sit quietly for 20 minutes thinking about what you really stand for. Write your observations in a journal and look at what you wrote for a week.*

27

19. Taking Responsibility

If we stop trying to be wise and intelligent, we will meet fewer "stupid" people.

If we stop insisting on kindness and compassion, we will encounter fewer "beggars."

If we accumulate less, and create fewer laws to protect it, there will be fewer "thieves."

Without intelligence, kindness, laws, and locks, what is there? The freedom to place ourselves, responsibly and responsively, at the center of things.

David Roth

————

"I CAN'T STAND IT, " the salesperson says. "My customers are so dumb!" "Why won't they let me help them? I know I'm right," says another. "They'll screw me if I give them half a chance!" says a third. Now listen to their customers. "He must think I'm an idiot." "She must think I'm helpless." "He's out to get me."

The same thing happens in our relationships away from work. "You're wrong." "That's stupid." "You don't care enough about me." "You ought to know how I feel without being told."

All anger is nothing more than the attempt to make someone feel guilty.

A COURSE IN MIRACLES

We can hardly expect strong people to welcome our attempts to control them. If nothing else, their self-respect may cause them to resist. And of course their resistance makes us angry. Our anger is both a mirror and a cruel dance. We use anger at others to express our unconscious discomfort at qualities within ourselves we aren't happy about. It's hard to accept weaknesses within ourselves, easier to attack them, secondhand, in others. The dance evolves when both parties in an angry relationship become skilled at doing exactly what drives the other person crazy.

Weak people play a similar game, accepting the criticism as a way of validating their own low self-image, and then repeating the behavior that made us angry in the first place, again, and again, and again.

Don't "should" on me and I won't "should" on you.

DAVID ROTH

德 *Think of a person who "makes you angry." Accept the fact that your anger is your response to the situation. You make yourself angry. Identify the actions within your control that contribute to the anger. Stop doing your part of it and notice what happens.*

20. BEING DIFFERENT

From the viewpoint of beliefs, all doubt is disastrous. From the viewpoint of faith, doubt is the indispensable stimulant.

FREDERICK FRANCK

As soon as we light a great fire and proclaim "This is right!" we create a dark shadow, "That is wrong." The fire is warm, attractive, and seductive. The fire is harmful, consuming, destructive. It hates the shadow.

Glorify light and you wind up cursing the dark.

Stop thinking about the best way to label things and people.

What is the real difference between light and dark? Between yes and no? Between good and evil? Between success and failure?

The most important labels to get rid of are the ones we put on ourselves, in comparison to other people.

———

OTHERS FOLLOW THE LATEST trend with enthusiasm. Should I run after them or rest peacefully where I am? Others appear to have a lot of money. Should I try to get more, or merely enjoy living with enough? Others are bright and witty. Should I struggle to imitate their speech or find my own voice? Others confidently carve out successful careers. Should I thrash about trying to reach some unclear destination, try to pattern my life after someone else's, or simply allow myself to move with the life developing around and within me?

The challenges of selling almost inevitably cause us to doubt ourselves from time to time, especially in today's world in which so much change comes so fast. We can deny the doubts (merely driving them into our subconscious mind) or acknowledge them as the first step in finding out what we really do believe and how we really should act.

Being "different" is scary only if we fail to look closely at the cost of being the "same." Allowing ourselves to feel, and then examine that fear, removes its power to hurt us.

德 *List on a piece of paper whatever "I should..."'s currently drive your actions and feelings. One at a time, change each of the "I should..."'s to "I choose to..." and notice what new actions and feelings open up for you.*

21 . FAITH

*When Jonathan Edwards wrote that we must "consent" to goodness, he meant
that we must trust in it, persevere in it, believe that our own good intentions will
be met with goodness in return—to have faith in the product and the customer.*

TOM CHAPPELL

The light of truth, or Tao, or God, is an inner radiance, not an
outward fire.

Its name is unknowable, so how can one grasp it? By letting go the
desire to know, name, or possess it.

It is dark and bottomless, so how can one embrace it? By allowing
one's self to be embraced by it.

It is, before the world was.

Limited as I am by human sight, hearing, and sense, how can I know
this?

Its secrets are written within me, plain to see if I let myself look.

---

*People can't live with change if there's not a changeless core inside them.
The key to the ability to change is a changeless sense of who you are, what
you are about and what you value.*

*If you start to think the problem is "out there," stop yourself. That
thought is the problem.*

STEPHEN COVEY

SELLING, LIKE EVERYTHING ELSE we do in life, can appear to be confusing, self-
defeating, uncertain. And yet, at the scariest, most perplexing times, we can
choose to have faith, whatever we understand that faith to be. Acting on that faith
means deciding what purpose our lives can accomplish and then following that
purpose. It is both a powerful and empowering choice. What's not always evident
is that it is a choice.

When things don't happen the way you wanted, instead of viewing them as
defeats or signs of failure, look for the "lesson" contained in the result. How could
you use that experience to grow? Treat life not as a sprint for a prize but as a long,
extended dance.

德 *Right now, list five losses, embarrassments, or "defeats" you have
experienced in the past month. (If you can't list any, are you
really committed to accomplish things with colleagues and clients?) Write
one positive learning from each situation. Use that new knowledge in some
productive way today.*

30

Practicing:

BECOMING CENTERED

1. **Live in the present**

Pay attention to where you are in each sales call. Are you thinking about what you want to say or do next, or anticipating the customer's next move and already planning your response? Are your thoughts preoccupied with what has happened in the past? Allowing the past and future to intrude on the present robs us of all the power we have in the moment when we are with the customer.

If you turn your focus on the customer instead of yourself, all the possibilities in the moment and the evolving relationship open up. Ask yourself:

- What's new in our relationship right now?
- What's my client feeling right now?
- How do I work with those feelings in a clear, caring way, instead of pushing my own agenda and dwelling on my own concerns, needs, or fears?

2. **Let go of expectations**

When you have to make a decision, instead of concentrating on what you know, ask yourself, "What don't I know?" Even better, ask someone else.

PETER SENGE

When you think you understand everything about a sales relationship with a customer, and clearly see the opportunity, ask yourself: "What is it about this person and situation which my expectations are causing me **not** to see? What am I missing?"

3. **Stop forcing things**

What we resist, persists

The same lesson works with resistance and opposition. When you believe you are completely blocked in a sales relationship, instead of pushing against the customer, ask the customer the same question: "I feel really stuck here. What am I missing?"

4. **Let go of control**

When you feel caught in a sales relationship that isn't productive, instead of yielding to the desire to take control of the situation in some way (or giving up), ask yourself: "What is it about the other person that I'm not willing to trust?" "What is it about **myself** that I'm not willing to trust?" Then give the trust that you want to receive in return. If you do this with integrity, you will not come to harm.

5. Suggest, don't "sell"

Share the success of the sales process with the customer. When you want to make a recommendation (or solve the customer's problem), **give the choice to the customer.** Instead of saying: "You should [then stating your solution or recommendation]...." or "You need to...." or "I recommend that you...." ask the question: "What do you think would happen if you [then state your solution or recommendation]. ...?" or "Suppose you ... [then state your solution or recommendation]?"

6. Accept the gifts your customer gives you

Pay more attention to what the customer is giving you. Work with those gifts, even if they don't seem like gifts, rather than in spite of them. The questions are simple: "What am I being given that has value to the customer? How can I work with that instead of against it?"

One of the greatest gifts we can receive is clear, honest feedback. Ask customers how you can do a better job providing service to them. If there's tension in the relationship, ask for insight into what you're doing that contributes to the tension. "I feel as if I'm pushing too hard here." "I feel like I'm getting in the way right now." "It feels like I'm moving too fast right now." "Can you help me out?" "Am I getting in the way?"

7. Give your own gifts freely and fully

At the close of each sales call, ask yourself: "What is the greatest gift I can give this customer right now?" Then give that gift simply, with no strings attached. Remember that your gift expresses your greatest value. Surely you are worth more than a nice pen, a fancy lunch, or tickets to a ball game.

Remember that the greatest gifts are personal gifts:

- Giving others your full, undivided attention.
- Listening fully and completely without interrupting.
- Accepting someone else's understanding of things without arguing for your way of thinking or belief.
- Acknowledging the goodness of what others have done without seeking to exploit it.
- Accepting feedback and even criticism without resistance—and thanking the other person for their gift to you.
- Helping others solve their own problems rather than positioning yourself as the expert.

Non-Doing

THE TAO INVITES US to see ourselves as free to choose, and not to feel "acted upon." That gift is available every day, every time something "good" happens to us, and especially when something "bad" takes place. The giver of that gift is patient and the gift is inexhaustible.

The sky was still blue, the sun still beaming when they locked me up. But during my incarceration it had begun to rain. The legendary Seattle rain. It was a thick gray rain; hard and fast and cold. In it, we had to walk four blocks from the Public Safety Building to the Ziller's Jeep—we were at its mercy. As was my custom in such elements, I hunkered against the rain, drew my head into my collar, turned my eyes to the street, tensed my footsteps and proceeded in misery. But my hosts, I soon noticed, reacted in quite another way. They strolled calmly and smoothly, their bodies perfectly relaxed. They did not hunch away from the rain but rather glided through it. They directed their faces to it and did not flinch as it drummed their cheeks. They almost reveled in it. Somehow, I found this significant. The Zillers accepted the rain. They were not at odds with it, they did not deny or combat it; they accepted it and went with it in harmony and ease. I tried it myself. I relaxed my neck and shoulders and turned my gaze into the wet. I let it do to me what it would. Of course, it was not trying to do anything to me. What a silly notion. It was simply falling as rain should, and I, a man, another phenomenon of nature, was sharing the space in which it fell. It was much better regarding it that way. I got no wetter than I would have otherwise, and if I did not actually enjoy the wetting, at least I was free of the tension. I could even smile.

TOM ROBBINS,
Another Roadside Attraction

Surrender in order to achieve.

Bend in order to stand tall.

Empty yourself in order to be full.

Die in order to be born.

Give all away in order to receive all.

These thoughts appear in the words of many religions and beliefs. We struggle against the paradoxes they express. We would do better to accept and act upon them. In the acceptance, the paradox disappears, in the action the complicated becomes simple.

––––––––––

IF, AS SALESPEOPLE, we don't blind our clients by who we say we are and what we say we know, they will see better and understand more. If we don't talk a lot, what we do say will be heard and respected. If we merge our goals with the client's, we will encounter less resistance. If we stop pushing, they will stop pushing back. If we don't insist on the sale, they will develop the courage to buy.

If we are anxious to succeed, however, our actions drown out our words. Whatever we may say, our actions shout: "I WANT THIS SALE!" "I NEED THIS ORDER!" "I HAVE TO EARN THIS COMMISSION!" "I NEED YOUR MONEY!" Small wonder that we often scare the hell out of our clients.

If we don't act as if we need the sale, we're more likely to get it. That lack of desire must be felt; it can't be faked.

Try replacing all these desires with a simple thought: "I want to create value for both of us. How can we find it together?" Repeat that thought to yourself every few minutes during each sales call, and especially when you feel anxious about success.

德 *List the values you want from the client. They will probably include things like: "commitment," "open communication," and "honesty." List the actions you would like from the client. If you move beyond the superficial "I want the client to buy what I sell," these actions will probably include: "keeping me informed about changes," "sharing bad news with me immediately," "confronting difficult issues together," "keeping promises," "respecting my time and my feelings."*

Make the decision to give these things to the client first, without being asked, and see what happens.

Say exactly what is needed in that moment and then be silent.

Do exactly what is needed in that moment and then be quiet.

Consider how it is in nature.

When the wind blows, it blows. Trees bend and crumpled things scurry in front of its force. When the storm is over, the wind stops.

Nature is efficient, truly economical. Human action is often incomplete, full of doubt, and wasteful.

Be like nature. Warm in the sunlight, wet in the rain. When it is time to grow, grow. When it is time to give, give. When it is time to act decisively, act. When the action is completed, stop.

––––––––

SALES CALLS HAVE THEIR own natural rhythm. That rhythm reflects the growth of trust between buyer and seller. Too often we ignore that rhythm, try to manipulate it, or inadvertently destroy it. Another paradox: we gain the ability to positively influence outcomes exactly when we stop trying, consciously, to do so. The best sales happen when we allow ourselves to act strongly and wisely in the moment to discover the best outcome which is already there in the relationship.

- Focus your first efforts on developing the ability to discuss needs and concerns freely with the customer. Stay on that level until the discussion feels honest and comfortable.
- Once you're comfortable talking about needs, work to help the customer better understand the meaning, value, and cost of these apparent needs. Stay at that level until the customer is clear about needs and excited about a solution.
- Agree about what the customer really cares about before even thinking about proposing a solution.
- Help the customer find a real solution to a real problem through what you offer. Keep checking the solution against the needs until the customer is convinced the solution is real.
- Help the customer develop the courage to act on the solution by working through the risks involved in implementation.

 In the next interpersonal situation in which you feel tension or anxiety, ask yourself, "What's really happening right now?"

Notice people trying to get something just beyond their reach. They strain and lose their balance.

Notice people in a hurry. They spend as much time backtracking as they do going forward.

If we try to define ourselves, that definition is limited by our fears and bounded by what we believe possible.

If we seek power over others, we lose it within ourselves.

If we allow our work to define our worth, we become its slave.

If you want to experience inner peacefulness, complete each day's work and let go.

———

AS SALESPEOPLE WE HEAR a lot about setting goals. The common mythology about sales performance, at least in the United States, is that to be motivated, a salesperson needs to be driven by external challenges: higher yearly sales goals and budgets, competitions, threats, bonuses and rewards. These stimuli do trigger actions, much as an electric shock will stimulate a cow, or an amoeba. The question is: are the actions in pursuit of these goals purposeful?

The answer is easier to state than to do because it requires a great deal of trust and faith. Take care of today as well as you can, and let go of it. Live in the present moment as fully as you can, and believe that these full moments will add up to a full week, a full month, a full year, a full life.

- Stop responding and start being. If you're living in a difficult time, then that's what you're faced with. Trying to change the conditions around you by acting in response to them only increases their power over you.
- Start trusting yourself. The deeper and more powerful your goals and values, the deeper and more powerful your actions.
- Let go of the desire to control. Awaken the strength to work with the flow of things, not against it.
- Create more calm inside yourself; act from within that calm and not according to the outward pressure.

德 *Think about a difficult interpersonal relationship. Ask yourself, "What's a better, more honest way to handle this situation?" Handle it right now.*

There was something formless and perfect
before the universe was born.
It is serene. Empty.
Solitary. Unchanging.
Infinite. Eternally present.
It is the mother of the universe.
For lack of a better name,
I call it the Tao.

STEPHEN MITCHELL

When we let go of the need to control, what can we trust? What is permanent?

Individuals die, but human life persists as a part of nature. Nature persists, within a universe we can't comprehend. The universe expands beyond our knowledge until it becomes the Tao.

———

THINK FOR A MOMENT of the meaning of the word "faithful." Trustworthy, dependable, full of faith. If we are the most permanent, stable thing in our universe, we are no stronger than our latest doubt. If we are no greater than our last success, any mishap can crush us. If we depend on others for our sense of well-being, a frown can shatter our happiness.

In a difficult, uncertain world, what stability do you bring to your customers? Merely your own? That's like throwing a drowning person a lifeline from the center of the whirlpool.

There is no such thing as a problem without a gift for you in its hands.
You seek problems because you need their gifts.

RICHARD BACH

We live in a time of extraordinary change and uncertainty. We live in a time of extraordinary spiritual renewal. The gift of these times is the ability to choose the purpose for which we live our lives.

In difficult times, it's understandable that people will pray for easier times—for themselves. As if God ran a daily lottery for peace of mind, financial security, and unconditional love. The truth is that we already have everything we need. Once we accept that truth, the way becomes clearer.

德 *Think about a current problem you're trying to resolve. Look for the gift contained in the problem. Act in ways that honor and acknowledge that gift.*

If we try to gain a sense of direction by following the changes around us, we are whirled into confusion. We become scattered and lost, as people and organizations.

Being rooted allows the willow to withstand the strongest winds.

Being centered allows us to move effortlessly with change yet constantly be in a calm, peaceful place.

————

None of us exist independent of our relationships with others. Different settings and people evoke some qualities from us and leave others dormant. In each of these relationships, we are different, new in some way.

MARGARET WHEATLEY,
Leadership and the New Science

How UNDERSTANDABLE, for us as salespeople, to want the world around us to stop moving, to become safe and predictable—the way we tell ourselves it used to be (it was moving then, just more slowly).

How understandable, for us as people, to blame our indecision and lack of direction on the forces outside us which we feel we can't control, any more than the tree controls the wind.

In times of change, we need to look inside ourselves to find our deepest roots and nourish them.

"But I'm a shallow person," someone told me once. "I have no roots."

When we tell ourselves that, we forget nature's wisdom. The smallest root, left to itself, knows how to search for rich, nourishing soil. The root is there. Let it start growing.

The ground which nurtures our roots includes our customers (and all the other people we care about); they are the soil in which we grow.

德 *List your four to five top customers. Identify what's special about them. For each customer, find a way, today, to let them know how much you value what they bring to the relationship. Next week, repeat the exercise with your next top four to five customers. Keep going.*

27. TRYING TO GET SOMEWHERE

"I'm trying to get somewhere in my life."
"I want things to be clearer, easier, simpler, happier than they are now."

Where is the "somewhere" we're trying to get to? How will we recognize it when we get there? Would we want to stay there once we got there? What makes us think it will be any better than where we are now?

The mind searches for a sense of direction; the spirit understands a sense of place.

The artist understands that the brush will find the painting that the eye can't see.

The scientist forgets theory in order to discover meaning.

Whatever changing situation or difficult person we find ourselves confronted by, that is where we can find our greatest strength. By asking always for ease and predictability, we nourish weakness.

The "somewhere" we really need to get to is the present moment, the place we need to arrive at is the here and now, with all its challenges and opportunities.

What is it about business that makes one forget that no matter how fast or how slow one goes, no matter how straight or meandering the path, all business people wind up in the same place, even if one gravestone happens to be bigger than another? There is only the journey to savor. The end is the same end for all of us.

MEL ZIEGLER

UNFULFILLED, EASILY DISCOURAGED salespeople seek easy customers to cling to. "Successful" salespeople know that the tough customers are their real job, and seek them out joyfully. Unfulfilled, easily discouraged salespeople want to get somewhere "better" than where they are. "Successful" salespeople have learned that where they are right now is the best possible world because it's the only real world they inhabit.

德 *If you find yourself in a hard place and wish to be "someplace else," whether it's a new relationship, or boss, or market, or job, ask yourself "What would I do differently if I were where I want to be?" Then start acting in that fashion where you are now.*

If you are confronted by a difficult customer, ask yourself "How do I act with those customers I feel comfortable with?" Then start treating the difficult customer the same way and notice what happens.

40

28. Technique and Wisdom

"If your only tool is a hammer,
pretty soon everything starts to look like a nail."

Technique and wisdom. Technique is "male," powerful, intrusive, commanding, rational. Wisdom is "female," enduring, encompassing, flowing, intuitive. That is why the masters knew the technique but followed wisdom.

Technique seeks to change things, wisdom to be at one with them as they evolve. Technique is personal, and says to the world, "Obey me." Wisdom is impersonal, and allows the world to be what it is.

Technique is the fire that burns; wisdom the light that illuminates.

When we try to control things with technique, the challenge changes in front of us faster than we can adapt. We struggle awkwardly with tools that won't shape, or smooth, or cut. But when we surrender to the flow of the work, the right tools spring effortlessly to our hands.

———

THERE ARE ONLY TWO SALES disciplines, just as there are two life disciplines. One is making each day a time for learning. "What is happening to me right now that I can learn from? How will this moment help me grow? How do I deepen my understanding of this situation I have just experienced? How can I sharpen my skills?"

The other is forgetting everything we have learned when we are face to face with the customer. Trust that the knowledge and skills we have inside us at that moment will be the best we can summon and draw upon in that moment. The more freely and confidently we use them, the better they'll work.

德 *Practice, in your next call, distinguishing between the messages that arise effortlessly out of the situation and the messages that are driven by insecurity. One message we experience in our actions, the other we hear in our minds. One message is truthful, the other is not. Let yourself flow as effortlessly as possible in the direction of what's true.*

Practicing:
Non-Doing

1. **Be silent**
   If you're "telling," you're not really "selling."

   JOHN HONE

The freedom to act with full spontaneity can be learned by "not-doing" what your habits and expectations tell you to do.

- When you feel the urge to speak, pause and be silent until the client speaks.

- When you feel the urge to solve a problem, ask the client for a solution.

- When you feel the urge to interrupt, continue listening.

- When you feel the urge to argue or contradict clients, support your clients' right to see things their way.

2. **Be clear**

Fear of what may happen often causes us to say too much, and we thus wind up saying nothing. "Suppose if I do this, the client will object, or dislike me, or question me, or get angry?" Often we beat around the bush and explain what we're going to say, until the message is completely blurred. Or we attempt to manipulate the conversation to lead the client to where we want the conversation to go—and both of us wind up lost. Or we doubt our own clarity and repeat ourselves. If we have gained a sense of calm purposefulness, we can start trusting our instincts. More to the point, we can start trusting the place those instincts come from. Say exactly what you mean as simply and concisely as possible, and then allow the client to work with it. Less talk; more meaning.

3. **Be balanced**

The same confusion happens when we swing between assertive and supportive behavior. "If I'm too assertive, I'll blow the sale." "If I'm too passive, I'll blow the sale." So we wind up in "no-man's land," neither fully assertive nor fully supportive—and often we blow the sale, anyway. Real balance is acting fully in the moment and not worrying about outcomes. If our actions are motivated by a genuine desire for collaboration and service, there is nothing to fear. Practice being more passionate about the values you most strongly believe in; let your whole self express the message. In the same sales meeting, practice being completely supportive—no ego at all. Pay attention to what happens so you can hone the skill of when to be firm and when to be caring.

4. **Ask for what you need**

A collaborative sales relationship is a two-way street between buyer and seller. For you to meet (or exceed) clients' expectations, you will probably need them to make commitments to you. These commitments might include complete, timely information, access to people and resources, clarity about their goals and intentions, and open discussion of their concerns and reservations. Not asking for what you need establishes unrealistic expectations and encourages poor teamwork between you and the client.

5. Confront difficult issues immediately

Even when you offer integrity, clarity, service, or partnership, not every client will choose to respond in kind. There are people so caught up in their own needs and fears that they can't get past them. If you are working with a client and know that they are asking you to do things that go against your values or best interests, surface that concern immediately, in descriptive, non-blaming, clear, compassionate language.

Practice the following simple model and integrate it into your own style:

> "In order for me to … [describe the value you would like to create for the client] … I need you to … [describe the specific behavior you'd like from the client to help make that happen]."

6. Get to the point

Some clients are unable to confront their own feelings or the consequences of their actions, and thus keep evading the issue. If you find yourself going back over the same ground with a client several times and continuously re-explaining your position, recognize that the problem has nothing to do with your position. You need to help the client come to terms with his or her actions. The following model, integrated into your own style, can help you and the client achieve greater clarity:

> "When you … [describe the specific behavior of the client that troubles you—without attacking the client] … I respond (or I feel, or I think) … [simply and concisely describe the effect of the other person's actions on you] … and that causes … [describe the negative effect on the positive relationship and business relationship you're trying to achieve]."

7. Invest your value wisely

If you believe working with a certain client will compromise the values you most strongly believe in, politely and immediately end the sales call or sales relationship. Your time, energy, and value are assets. Invest them with the clients that will increase the worth of these assets. Working with clients who aren't willing to collaborate or cooperate may generate cash flow, but these clients strip the value, and thus the profits, from your business.

IT'S HARD FOR WESTERNERS, especially Americans, to understand the Taoist principle of wu-wei, "non-acting" action. The notion flies in the face of what selling is supposed to be all about.

It helps to think of wu-wei as "effortless" action. The action still takes place, but gracefully, spontaneously, without conscious thought or intention. The person acting has passed from doing to simply being the action. Wu-wei is the harmony of body, mind, and spirit, in which the actor disappears into the act itself.

The greatest athletes in our society know this relaxed fusion of self and action, and accept the paradoxes that go into developing mastery of their particular sport.

At the root of mastery is patient, persistent practice of basic skills. If you want to get a top professional like Michael Jordan really upset, talk about his "natural ability" or "God-given talent." He'll tell you about thousands of hours shooting baskets. And the point of practice is the ability to perform under pressure without conscious thought, to let the shot "shoot itself," rather than shooting it.

The great athletes not only practice, they prepare. Much has been written about the incorporation of meditation and visualization into how champion athletes prepare for a game or contest. They integrate within themselves the best performance of which they are capable, and then, in the event itself, allow that high level of performance to "do" itself.

One paradox is to forget everything that has been learned, practiced, and prepared and be "one" with the moment of doing. Bill Russell described some of the legendary battles between the Celtics and Lakers in terms of "no time." Time and consciousness just ceased to exist. There was only the flow of moment to moment.

In the state of "non-doing," perception changes. The tennis ball looks as big as a pumpkin. The great hitters "see" the seams rotating on a baseball thrown at 90 m.p.h. Or, as Michael Jordan says, "The net looks as big as Lake Michigan."

The other paradox with great athletes in team sports is the suspension of ego. It's not that they don't have strong egos; just that the ego is put aside when it's time to play. With the surrender of ego comes flexibility and versatility. If the shot is falling easily, keep shooting. If it's not, keep shooting anyway, because it will, or stop shooting, and concentrate on passing, or rebounding, or playing defense.

The Tao floats and soars.
It can go left or right.

Come to think of it, maybe Michael Jordan is like the Tao.

Win/Win

"I used to pride myself on my negotiating skill. I made sure I swept the table clean of every loose penny that was around. It never occurred to me that winning big could be a negative thing. At the time, it felt great: business is a competitive sport, and I just cleaned the table! After I left EDS, I learned that sometimes it's better to leave something on the table. Sometimes you do better if you leave people alternatives. You do better if your customer or your competitor doesn't feel taken advantage of. You do better, in fact, if your customer feels like your partner."

MORT MEYERSON
CEO, PEROT SYSTEMS

There is a time for being ahead,
a time for being behind;
a time for being in motion,
a time for being at rest;
a time for being vigorous,
a time for being exhausted;
a time for being safe,
a time for being in danger.

STEPHEN MITCHELL

———

SALES NEGOTIATIONS PRESENT special challenges because of the financial and emotional impulse to "win." What gets lost in the act of winning, however, is the cost of victory, not only in the long term, but in the immediate deal itself. In reality, nobody "wins" a win/lose negotiation. By the time both parties have battled through grudging concessions wrung painfully from mistrust and resistance, most of the real profit is gone from the deal. And the residue is punishing: the losing party seeks revenge, even at the cost of their best business interests.

In a successful long-term sales relationship, "wins" and "losses" diminish in scope and even out over time. More important, the added value gained by creative collaboration puts more money on the table, for both parties to share, than could ever be gained in a hostile win/lose competition.

Sometimes as salespeople we have to negotiate with buyers who aren't interested in "win/win" at all. These are the buyers who proudly display the sign "I shoot every third salesperson, and the second one just left." These are the buyers whose vocabulary starts and ends with "No," and whose idea of a clarifying question is "What part of 'No' don't you understand?"

德 *In your next negotiation with a "tough" customer, deliberately and obviously leave something on the table because you **want** to, not because you were forced to.*

46

30. PERSUASION

Every forceful action produces an opposite counter-force. Violence begets revenge, pressure begets resistance, surrender begets aggression, "right" begets "wrong," "wrong" creates the desire for "right." Persuasion creates skepticism.

The truly powerful person does what is needed in the moment and then stops. Knowing that the universe will always pursue its own way, and thus be uncontrollable, such a person stops trying to dominate events, to bend people to an idea, to gain approval.

MOST SALESPEOPLE HAVE BEEN taught that their goal is to persuade others, to change people's minds, to force agreement, to motivate people to do something they hadn't originally intended. In negotiations, as in selling, persuasion sends a signal to many customers that they are "under attack." Of course they resist.

Persuasion typically begins with the promises we make to customers.

- "This widget (or program, or strategic plan, or training program) will solve all your problems."
- "They'll love this. Morale and productivity will soar."
- "If you make this change, profits will increase 150 percent and you'll drive your competition out of business."
- "These machines never break down."
- "You'll be able to install this by yourself. An idiot could do it."
- "This new launch will be a blockbuster."
- "You'll get a lot of use out of this—it's state of the art."
- "That color looks just marvelous on you."
- "This season's Gift With Purchase will have people beating down your doors."

Having made the promise, we then work like crazy to manage the outcomes—or run like hell and hope the client's check clears fast. After all, we're on commission, aren't we?

Rethink the point and value of "persuasion." If you persuade your customers to take risks, are you willing to run these risks with them? If you aren't willing to risk your support, how can you expect them to risk their commitment? If you aren't being straightforward with them, what do you expect in return?

德 *Write down the promises you made this week. How many did you keep? Intend to keep? Call at least one customer right now and realign expectations so they're real.*

47

31. DOING WHAT IS NEEDED IN THE MOMENT

Weapons are the tools of violence;
all decent men detest them.

STEPHEN MITCHELL

If it is time for war, then engage in war, but do so with great power and equally great restraint.

Winning the battle and losing the war is bad tactics. Winning the war and losing the peace is bad strategy.

Why hate your enemies? They are only human like yourself. Hatred is the mind's trick that allows us to forget that in harming others, we attack ourselves.

Enter the battle gravely, with sorrow and great compassion, as if you were attending a funeral. If we recognized that in killing others we kill ourselves, we would take less pleasure in it.

———

"DOING WHAT IS NEEDED IN THE MOMENT" means at times taking actions that we know will harm others.

"Doing what is needed in the moment" means taking business away from a supplier, saying "No" to a customer, refusing to act on someone's passionate demand or emotional request.

"Doing what is needed in the moment" means that one's success can cause pain to others. It's very human to want to avoid that pain, or to numb ourselves to it so we can pretend it doesn't exist, or to nourish our anger so that inflicting pain on others feels justified. It's also very destructive.

德 *Think of a customer whom you believe you really want to say "No" to but can't bring yourself to confront. Let go of your anxiety. Decide to say "No" not as an act of violence against the other person but as a way of affirming your positive beliefs. Make the commitment to confront your issue with him or her as clearly and compassionately as possible.*

Think of a customer whose resistance makes you angry. Let go of the anger. Chances are you are causing at least half of the resistance by your own behavior. Practice stating your position fairly, simply, and calmly.

32. FREEDOM FROM OUR BELIEFS AND HABITS

If powerful men and women
could remain centered in the Tao,
all things would be in harmony.
The world would become a paradise.
All people would be at peace,
and the law would be written in their hearts.

STEPHEN MITCHELL

———

The warrior Tsukahara Bokuden, founder of The Way of Winning Without Trying, was accosted by a burly, loudmouthed bully while on a boat trip to eastern Japan. Hearing of Bokuden's school of martial arts, the bully challenged him to a duel. Quietly signaling the boatman to land on a deserted islet, Bokuden accepted the challenge. The bully jumped immediately ashore, drew his long sword, and shouted, "Come on, come on! I'll split your skull in two!" Still aboard the boat, Bokuden put aside his swords, picked up the boatman's pole, and shoved the boat out into the water, stranding the bully. "Now you understand Winning Without Trying," he said. "If you want a lesson for the road, swim out here and get it!"

VIOLENCE TOWARD OTHERS begins in our own feelings of powerlessness. We attack out of our own perceived weakness. Then we invent rationales to mask that weakness.

Practice listening to your own thinking as you express it in words:

"We have to do it this way...."

"But that's always been our policy...."

"Top management would never agree to that change...."

"I have no choice...."

"This is how I've always sold...."

"If I give in, they'll walk all over me...."

"If I'm not tough, they'll never respect me...."

When we allow our beliefs and habits to dictate our actions, we surrender the freedom to act in ways that bring harmony and goodness to our lives and the lives of others. We also wind up leaving much too much money on the table in negotiations.

德 *Describe one of your toughest customer relationships to a friend or trusted colleague. Invite the other person to listen for an opportunity your beliefs are preventing you from recognizing, feeling, or hearing. Accept whatever is given you without resistance.*

49

33. Manipulation

Clever people know how to manipulate things.

Harmful people know how to manipulate other people.

Wise people know merely themselves.

Therefore, seek not to master things or other people, but yourself.

Let go of the desire to possess the world to make yourself whole. Wholeness is within.

THINK ABOUT HOW YOU NEGOTIATE. What is the intention behind what you do? To manipulate the customer? To satisfy your own ego? To keep from being harmed by someone you perceive as being more powerful?

It has been said that our words form only 7 percent of the complex messages we send others, our tone of voice 38 percent, and our nonverbal expression 55 percent. That means that at some level, customers pick up the messages we send, especially when they are of domination or fear. Customers know, at some level, if they are being treated with straightforward honesty or if they are being manipulated. The feeling may not take conscious form—"This person's just out to get me!"—but the customer will sense the attack and respond with aggressiveness or defensiveness.

Manipulative tactics only make the matter worse because they confirm the customer's suspicion. They send the message "I don't trust you to be fair, and I don't trust myself, either."

If you feel and communicate the message "No harm," and act in strong, open, fair ways, you create opportunities for success with customers. Help them question their own goals and solutions, expand their sense of what is possible and clarify their awareness of outcomes, not as an expert, or an opponent, merely as a friend.

德 *The next time you negotiate, imagine that there are two negotiations going on: the "outer" one is verbal, the exchange of demands and offers. The other, "inner" negotiation is emotional—the balancing of self-respect. If we insist on beating the other person, we will attack their power and sense of self-esteem. They will resist instinctively, even at the cost of what could have been a good agreement. Practice letting them "win" the inner negotiation of trust and self-esteem so you can make progress on the outer deal itself. It's like playing chess on two stacked transparent boards, in which the goal is to win the game on both boards, but vertically, not horizontally.*

Tao stretches through time and space, unbeginning and unending. How unlike our sense of human life—so full of starts and stops and unclear choices, troubling us with so many little deaths before the final end.

Tao seeks to possess nothing because it is in all things. Because it isn't possessive, powerful people, whose lives are driven by the need to possess, disdain it, failing to notice the ground over which they carelessly, purposelessly, and in the end, frantically hurry.

WHERE DO WE FIND OUR STRENGTH, our source of power in negotiating? If we take pride in what we know, we build a house on shifting sands. "Knowledge" changes daily; if we look, we always can find people smarter than ourselves.

Because power is energy, it needs to flow ... it cannot be confined. What gives power its charge, positive or negative, is the quality of relationships. Those who relate through coercion, or from a disregard for the other person, create negative energy. Those who are open to others and who see others in their fullness create positive energy.

MARGARET WHEATLEY

If we draw strength from our power to give commands, reward people, instill fear, and court favorites, we sow, reap, and eat a poisoned harvest. Power breeds envy, commands make people helpless, rewards cripple independence, and purchased loyalty constantly seeks a higher bidder.

If we use our ability to harm the customer as a source of power, we also create anger, resistance, and, ultimately, sabotage. Customers we have forced into a "bad" deal start undoing that deal, one way or another, as soon as it's closed.

The real power in negotiation comes from the energy between buyer and seller. It has much less to do with status and organizational title than we imagine. It has even less to do with ego. We still operate in a business culture that often treats negotiation as a kind of "Testosterone Olympics" in which the prize goes to the one who can make "the other guy blink."

德 *The next time you're in a "face down" with a customer, say, "You may be right. I hadn't thought about it that way. If you were to design a 'win/win' solution to this problem, what would it be?" Stay open to whatever the customer tells you. Act in ways that will benefit you and the other person.*

For someone centered in the Tao, there are no surprises and no danger, only peacefulness, even in a world filled with uncertainty and pain.

Without that peacefulness, every turn in the road of life offers new distractions, disappointments, and dangers.

The words that one uses to describe the Tao are dull and unexciting. Look and you see nothing; listen and you hear nothing. It is neither a map for navigating the future nor a weapon to fight off danger.

Yet it is in you, inexhaustible and trustworthy.

———

A successful general first wins, and then engages in battle; a losing general first engages in battle, and then hopes to win.

SUN TZU

WIN/LOSE NEGOTIATIONS BEGIN in posturing and defensiveness, proceed through closed or misleading communication to grapple blindly with poorly understood goals and needs, mistrust, and partial commitments. "Look. We need to get everything out on the table here. You start." "I agree. We need to cut to the chase and discuss real needs. You go first."

Our fear of being hurt at the end of the deal by something we didn't anticipate causes us to dig in, withhold information, and be less than open about our intentions. Small wonder that we get exactly the same in response.

If you make the commitment to creating a deal that is fair for both parties, then you always have the right to walk away from the table, right up to the last minute. If you keep the commitment, then the value the other side gains from an open exchange of possible "win/win" solutions will keep them at the table; they will have too much to lose to allow you to walk away.

Free from the fear of being surprised or harmed, you can work with openness, creativity, and real strength. Either there is a deal that represents real value for both parties or there isn't. Real strength also allows you to deal with the most aggressive customer calmly, purposefully, and successfully.

德 *Think of a customer relationship that isn't working. Call the customer up right now, and in your own words, say, "This isn't working. We have to find a better way or I can't continue to support what we're doing." Then be silent and let the customer come to terms with the situation.*

Practicing:

WIN/WIN

1.   Go in prepared

Our fear of losing a negotiation often causes us to act in ways that hurt both the customer and ourselves: generating distrust by not being clear about positions, making obvious concessions grudgingly, so that all the leverage is gone from them by the time they're surrendered, even acting in bad faith. We can protect ourselves against this fear by preparation:

- Know exactly what you absolutely must gain from the negotiation and why that goal is important to you.
- Know what you can reasonably afford to give away in order to get what you absolutely need, not merely what you might want.
- Know what the cost will be to you if you and the customer don't create a fair, workable agreement.
- Do the same preparation for what you believe will be the customer's positions.

2.   Be easy on people and tough on positions

Remember that there are two negotiations: one over the deal itself and one over respect and self-esteem. The more self-esteem you confer to the customer, the more you'll be able to gain in the deal.

3.   Stay open

Since you are interested only in an agreement that is reasonable and fair for both sides, the basic principle is that "everything is open until everything is finally closed." All concessions and interim agreements are subject to a final test for fairness and commitment. That means that, in perfectly good faith, you can make provisional concessions based on how the entire agreement ultimately works out. Make sure you tell the customer that's how you will be negotiating.

4.   Focus first on broad goals and consequences

Haggling over details at the start of a negotiation can kill trust and collaboration. Resist the impulse to start talking details until you've explored the customers' goals in a relaxed, open manner. Make sure you examine the customer's assumptions and expectations in depth. Even better, help customers examine their own assumptions and expectations.

5.   Make haste slowly

Listen, support, confirm, explore—before assuming anything. Share as much information as possible about your broad goals and your criteria for an acceptable deal. The fact that "everything's open until everything is finally closed" means you can't be trapped by sharing information.

If you find yourself caught up in positional haggling, stop. Table the issues you can't yet agree on and move to an area where there's likely to be reasonable progress. Use the collaborative success you create as positive energy when you go to tackle the tougher issues.

6.   Work toward "both/and" not "either/or"

When you encounter an impasse, instead of resisting, reframe the "either/or" obstacle as a creative challenge for both of you to solve. "How can we get **both** what you want **and** what I want?" If you have to say "No" to an offer or demand, remember to continue to support the possibility of a fair solution:

- "Let's find another way to do this...."

- "I can't say 'yes' to what you're asking. Surely we're capable of coming up with a better alternative."

- "I'd hate to see us lose what we've accomplished so far because we can't resolve this issue. What have we overlooked?"

7.   Be prepared to walk away

The better the potential "win/win" deal for customers, the more they have to lose by intransigence at the end. Use the positive momentum of the deal and the pain of losing everything as a way to get resistant customers to make a final commitment. Because you are committed to a mutually fair deal, you have the right to change concessions, take items off the table, or wipe the entire slate clean and restart from zero.

My friend and mentor, the late Leon Labes, has been credited with having invented the practice of "win/win" decades before it became popular, in a long and distinguished career as a labor lawyer. He put it this way: "You have to be fair and tough. They complement, not contradict each other. The more the other side believes in your absolute commitment to fairness, the tougher you can bargain. 'Fairness' isn't weakness, or stupidity. It's still a negotiation; the results count for something. But fairness is the way you get the results. Toughness is how you get the other side to be fair."

No Struggle

THERE ARE THREE DANGEROUS divisions that can trouble people's spirits and separate them from harmony and peacefulness. The first is the division between "me" and "you" worked out in clashes of will and desire in all our business and personal relationships. The second is the division between "me" and "it," the willed separation from the natural world that allows us to destroy and pollute the very world we need in order to survive. In cutting ourselves off from the relationship with the natural world, we also isolate ourselves from the wisdom of that world placed in it by its creator. The final division, of course, is between us and our own nature.

If we accept these divisions as permanent and real, our only choices are to pretend that "not me" has no reality, to ignore its existence, or to fight against it trying to extinguish it. The Tao invites us to see what we perceive as opposites to be both opposites and one at the same time.

> For to say that opposites are polar is to say much more than that they are far apart: It is to say that they are related and joined—that they are the terms, ends, or extremities of a single whole. Polar opposites are therefore inseparable, like the poles of the earth or of a magnet, or the ends of a stick or the faces of a coin.
>
> ALAN WATTS

You can sense this right now, if you wish, by spending a minute or so observing the back of your right hand. Note the texture, color, and shape of the back of your hand. As you look at it in its entirety, imagine the years that have created what you are looking at. If possible, visualize the blood coursing through the veins. Now turn your hand over and look at your palm. See the difference? See the oneness?

> But once the realization is accepted that even between the closest human beings infinite distance continues to exist, a wonderful living side by side can grow up, if they succeed in loving the distance between them which makes it possible for each to see the other whole and against a wide sky.
>
> RANIER MARIA RILKE

56

When we become more aware of how things work in the world we discover the truth of opposites:

To make something shrink, you first have to stretch it;

To weaken something, first allow it to become strong;

For something to fall, it first needs to stand up;

To diminish something, first give to it in abundance.

In time the soft and weak overcomes the hard and powerful. Therefore, real strength comes in understanding how things work. "Learn to see things backwards, inside out, and upside down."

JOHN HEIDER

In battle, combat is engaged directly with force, but victory is gained by surprise. Therefore the masters of the unpredictable are infinitely powerful, like heaven and earth, and inexhaustible as rivers. When they come to an end, they start again, like the cycle of days and months. When they die, they are reborn like the seasons.

SUN-TZU

Practicing "opposites":

- If you are meeting with a customer who is very aggressive, instead of responding defensively, or with even more aggressiveness, be polite, calm, and unconcerned.

- If your customer uses friendliness as a tactic to gain concessions, be serious and professional.

- If the customer is very knowledgeable, and uses knowledge like a weapon, appear ignorant and continue asking questions.

- If you're stuck in the past, refocus the discussion on future benefits to be gained.

- If the customer is worried about the future, point out the strengths of your past relationship.

- If the customer is stuck on small details, refocus on the big picture.

- If the customer is unfocused about goals and consequences, select a single critical incident to use as a test case.

 The next time you feel pressured to act in a certain way, do the opposite—simply, caringly, and calmly—and note what happens.

37. COMMON SENSE

The problem with "common sense" is it's not very common.
HENRY DAVID THOREAU

The world generates countless opposites; the Tao is itself, whole and complete. The world is busy; the Tao is calm. The world is frantically pursuing results; the Tao seeks nothing and yet leaves nothing undone.

If people could understand this, they would "do" much less and accomplish much more. Free from the push and pull of desire, the balance that their efforts constantly undo would seek to establish itself on its own.

The Tao teaches that we can trust our "common sense," the awareness present in all things, including ourselves, of what is purposeful and sensible. Only our desires block us from that awareness.

LETTING GO OF THOSE DESIRES can be as simple as questioning the things we believe we want.

- What do I want?
- Where does that desire come from? Am I, in fact, meeting someone else's agenda?
- What would getting that mean to me?
- Why is that goal important?
- What perceived emptiness in me am I expecting my desire to fill?
- What am I paying to get it?
- What could I seek to accomplish that would be more in keeping with my deepest values?

These are also good questions to help your customers ask themselves.

These questions are best explored in a quiet, calm place and time. If possible, select a time when you can relax completely, and listen attentively to the messages you receive. Remember, the "you" that asks the questions and listens thoughtfully to the answers is your conscious self and the "you" that responds to these questions speaks with the voice of the Tao.

德 *Identify a major desire, concern, or worry. Ask the questions above until you have greater clarity. Discuss your insights with a friend and pay attention to the feedback you receive. Act on these insights immediately.*

38. RULES AND ASSUMPTIONS

The wisest leaders don't worry about acting "wisely" because they recognize that "wisdom" represents what we have told ourselves about the past and what we imagine the future will be: partial memories solidified into "fundamental principles" and fond hopes turned into "immutable laws."

The most moral leaders do not practice "morality" because they know that what people call "morality" is often merely a justification for getting what they think they want. "Immorality," therefore, is just a convenient label for those who oppose them.

When people lose sight of the truth of things they have to turn, instead, to being "virtuous." When "virtue" doesn't work, they turn to "kindness." When "kindness" fails, then people rely on being "ethical." When "ethics" collapse, people start writing rules for others to obey and creating punishments for them when the rules are inevitably challenged and broken.

———

IT SEEMS STRANGE TO CONSIDER living life or running a business without rules. The assumption is that without rules, everything becomes chaos. "But if you don't have rules," a manager said to me once, "then you wind up with the monkeys running the zoo." What one sees, however, is that the rules, blindly written and blindly followed, create chaos or, at best, organized despair.

Our common sense tells us that when we say to ourselves, "But this policy is wrong! Why do we have to apply that restriction to this situation? It just doesn't make sense!"

Learning how to challenge rules and assumptions, therefore, becomes a growth step for people and organizations. It's neither practical nor wise to insist that our "rules" are simply better than other people's, or that their thinking is flawed, stupid, or doomed to failure. We can expect resistance to that message. If the questioning comes from a quiet, caring place inside us, others are more likely to be able to hear the message. If we speak from feelings of anger or helplessness, our words will be drowned out by our emotion.

Within the most rigid rule may be a simple principle of common sense. Instead of worrying about breaking the rule, find and act on the common sense principle.

No urgency, no force, no pressure. Let go of the telling; allow the discovery.

德 *List two to three of your basic "unwritten rules" about other people. (Clue: they will be triggered in your thinking by the words "always" and "never.") Think in an open way about your experience with people until you find at least one exception. The next time you think "always" or "never," ask yourself, "Is this another exception?"*

59

How things work:

Light penetrates darkness, growing plants reach through earth and stone for the sun, the earth balances itself, spinning in its dance of gravity through space.

The forest fire's heat splits the long-dormant seed and awakens the new tree. The predator keeps the herd strong—the stronger the herd, the more skilled the predator. Marsh becomes field, field becomes forest.

Suppose this balance did not exist in nature? What does it cost us when we ignore it in our own lives?

TANDA FOX WHO WORKED as a sales executive for Estée Lauder tells the story of shopping for a new car. She arrived at the dealership and was met by a salesperson who patiently and attentively explored with her what she was looking for. At no time did he offer to "sell" her a car. After about 30 minutes, he recapped what she'd identified as her needs and desires, and then invited her to test drive a car which matched those needs and desires.

They drove for about two minutes. The salesperson sat in the front seat, polite, attentive, saying absolutely nothing. Finally, the silence got to her and she had to ask a question: "Aren't you going to tell me anything about this car's features?" she asked. "Sure," he said, in the same air of polite concern. "What would you like to know?" This continued for about ten minutes as she gradually relaxed with him until all her questions were answered.

They came back to the showroom and, as they were getting out of the car, he said "It sounds like this is exactly the right car for you." "Absolutely," she replied. "Then let's go buy it," said the salesperson.

When she entered his office she saw two walls filled with plaques and awards. Not only was he the leading Porsche/Audi salesperson in the United States; he was their top salesperson in the world.

The greatest value we bring clients is this sense of how things work: creating balance by helping them question their own goals and solutions, expanding their sense of what is possible, clarifying their awareness of outcomes, but not as an expert, or an opponent, merely as a friend.

德 *Find a way to "do" the story above in your next client meeting.*

40. Confronting "Bad News"

What do we hear when we stop straining to listen?

What do we notice when we stop straining to see?

What do we feel when we let go our grasp?

What happens when we stop doing?

WHEN THINGS GO WRONG with a customer or client, the normal tendency is often to avoid the problem, or blame others. That's especially true when customers or clients confront us in anger about the problem. Our anxiety, fueled by our desires and fears, can cause us to miss and misinterpret messages completely.

"No news" is usually "bad news." If you have done something to cause a problem with a customer, or if something's gone wrong inside your company, bring it up immediately. The biggest problem is usually rooted in the salesperson's anxiety about confronting trouble with the customer and finding a way to make it right. Our guilt gets in the way. Meanwhile, the customer needs a solution. That's the real message. Getting caught up in emotion makes this solution harder to find and implement. If confronting bad news with customers is difficult, simplify the action.

- Call the customer as soon as you know there's a problem. The sooner you call, the easier it will be to deal with the issue. Before you call, get the facts, and sketch out the available options.

- Explain the problem without going into extensive detail about why it happened. Resist the opportunity to blame or get defensive. It happened. What matters is remedying the situation. If the problem was caused internally, briefly explain how your company will act to resolve the problem in the future. Long explanations usually fuel customers' powerlessness and anger because you suggest that customers don't know what you're doing. Most long explanations are usually the salesperson's way of trying to get rid of anxiety and embarrassment anyway.

- Give customers a choice. "We can ship part of the order now and the rest later, or send you a substitute and adjust your account accordingly. Which works best for you?" Helping customers focus on what they can do restores their sense of power and self-esteem.

德 *Identify a potential service or implementation issue within your organization that may cause problems for your customers. Go to the people involved right now, and work cooperatively with them to find a way to make service better and easier. If you know there's a serious problem and haven't notified the customer, do it now.*

41. RESISTANCE AND AWARENESS

A thoughtful, sensitive person becomes aware of how things work and
seeks to increase that awareness. An experienced, intelligent person
turns this knowledge into rules to follow, and promptly gets lost.
A practical, ambitious person hears of the way and laughs at it.

———————

IF, AS WE PRACTICE AWARENESS, we look for approval and confirmation
from others, we are bound to be disappointed. People who believe in rules will
call our flexibility irrational; people who believe in control will criticize our
giving as surrender. When we are silent, talkative people will call us dumb;
when we are inactive, aggressive people will label us weak and seek to use that
perceived weakness against us.

The unexpected frightens people. When our actions don't fit other people's
expectations or conform to their beliefs, they become threatened. Their resistance
and opposition is how they handle their fear.

If we do not push back against their resistance, it will more easily diminish
on its own.

德 *The next time you encounter resistance from a customer, regardless
of how you have handled similar situations with that person in
the past, make the choice not to respond or react initially.*

*Listen calmly to the objection or criticism. As you listen, allow
yourself to acknowledge that while this point of view may not be yours, it
certainly is theirs. If appropriate, allow yourself to nod and even smile, as
you would hearing the concern of a friend. Create as much space for the
other person as possible. You simply do not need to jump in and argue. If
you believe strongly in your point of view, it will make itself clear and
persuasive.*

*When the customer is finished, be silent for a moment. Allow the
energy to subside a little. Then restate the concern as simply and clearly as
possible, using the customer's own words as much as you can. Become quiet
again and note the response. You will be able to work productively with
whatever happens next.*

*Think through this scenario until you feel prepared, and then call a
customer with whom you're experiencing difficulties. Make the call today.*

42. TENSION AND SYNERGY

What is reality if it does not have to do with things, accomplishments, rational thought, or rules? We can think of it, as so many others have done, as a natural and spiritual process, present everywhere, in the world but not of the world.

Earlier civilizations expressed this process in numbers, which they understood not merely as abstract entities for counting things, but as symbols of the order within the universe.

Zero: Nothingness, a complete circle enclosing emptiness, a principle we can acknowledge but not know. St. Augustine described God as "A circle whose center is everywhere and whose circumference is nowhere."

One: Unity, the "oneness" of all creation, the desire to be "as one" with others. We lose this "oneness" at birth. Some people fight against the resulting loneliness all their lives.

Two: Duality, opposites, contradiction, tension, separation, the way we often experience life—Parent/Child, Female/Male, Brother/Sister—different cultures, religions, politics and personal beliefs—Plan/Actualization, Control/Freedom, Logic/Intuition, Order/Chaos, Good/Bad. Because the experience of duality is uncomfortable, even scary, some people deny its existence; others seek to eradicate those who are different from them.

Three: The creative union of opposites, Female + Male = Child

---

WHAT IS THE REAL VALUE OF SELLING and negotiating if it is not truly creative? Seller and buyer are opposites. We can begin the creative process by allowing them to be what they are, and recognizing our independence from them. The tension between us and them is not really harmful. It just is.

While acknowledging and respecting our differences, we can also look past them for those values we share in common and seek to deepen that mutual awareness. And from the merging of opposites—seller and buyer—comes creative growth: something of value that did not exist before.

德 *Think of a customer or client you would like to be doing more business with, but can't seem to "sell." Identify what it is that makes that client special and unique. Then identify what strong values you share in common. (If you don't know the answers to these questions, spend your next conversations with the client finding out.) As simply and naturally as possible, tell the client why you think he or she is special—without putting the "hit" on for a sale. Notice what opens up in the relationship.*

Practicing:
NO STRUGGLE

Recognize that most techniques for handling objections, or negotiating with difficult customers, actually **increase** resistance because they threaten customers, or make them look dumb. Instead of aggressive techniques, practice the art of "Winning by Not Resisting." All these techniques are grounded in a calm, empathetic regard for the customer, rather than hostility or suspicion. All rely on deep, active listening and patient observation without judgment. You will need to adapt each of these techniques to your own personal, natural style.

1.   Silence
Silence is often called "Zen Mind" or "Beginner's Mind." It is practiced by releasing all thoughts, especially fears, and allowing the client to speak when the client is ready. Often, if we respond to resistance with polite, attentive silence, the client will start working toward greater clarity and agreement by providing the missing information we need.

Silence is accompanied by quiet observation. Develop the ability not of staring at the customer, but becoming aware of the full space around the customer. Silence is supported by deep, relaxed, full breathing.

2.   Mirror
Reflect back the client's concerns or resistance, using the client's language, as a gentle, non-aggressive question. "We already use another vendor." "You already use another vendor?" Keep the technique simple and natural, and the client will explain the thinking and assumptions behind the concern or clarify the objection. Notice that this technique is not an interrogation. If you ask "Why do you use that vendor?" or other probing questions, it's easy for a client to perceive your question as an attack and start justifying the decision. Be patient. Learn.

3.   The Willow
When confronted with a demand you don't want to say "Yes" to, the natural response is to say "No." Of course, your resistance stimulates counter-resistance on the client's part. Instead, agree with the demand **in principle**. Then ask the client to consider the consequences if you did what he or she asked. Be flexible like the willow in a storm. "Sure, I suppose we could do that. How would we handle [state the negative consequences?]"

4.   The Stone (Wrapped in Silk)
If the customer asserts a belief you know is wrong or based on inaccurate assumptions, the temptation is to say, "But you're wrong! Let me set you straight." It's amazing how few customers appreciate being told they're incorrect, misinformed, or stupid. Instead, calmly state a solid fact that contradicts the customer's belief, in as supportive a manner as possible. "You may be right. Our information says that ... [state the contrary fact.]" "I know lots of people who believe that. In fact ... [state the contrary fact.]" "I can see why that might

be appealing to you. What we're seeing a lot more frequently is ... [state the contrary fact.]" No energy at all. Say it simply and step away from it.

5. The River

The river flows past obstacles or over them. When a customer makes a proposal you don't want to accept, acknowledge the proposal and immediately invite the customer to think of another way to solve the problem. No resistance; just flow. "That's one way. What's another?" "How else could we do it?"

6. The Cloud

Customers often get so caught up in their beliefs, assumptions, and fears, that they box themselves into a corner. "I have no time." "I have no resources." "I have no budget." Often these are ways of saying "I have no courage." "I have no faith in my ability (or trust in yours)." "The Cloud" is a way to redirect customers who are stuck into a desirable, hypothetical future, where the difficulties of the present don't exist. Begin by genuinely acknowledging their concern. "So it sounds like money is really tight." "You're really strapped for resources, aren't you?" "That's a full plate. It must be hard sorting through all those priorities."

Then ask the customer to speculate what he or she might do if the present obstacles **didn't** exist. "If there were a way to ... [state a goal you both want] what might it be?" "If there **were** one priority you would really like to achieve, what might it be?" "If money were no object, what would you like to do?" Once the goal is clear, and you've discussed the benefits to the customer of achieving that goal, then creatively discover how to achieve the goal within the real-world limits facing the customer.

7. The Fire

"The Fire" burns through what used to be called "hidden" or "false" objections. If a customer is resisting your attempts to develop your point of view (for example the value of a slightly better, but more expensive, level of service), name the issue you think is the sticking point for the customer. "So it sounds like price really is the most important consideration for you." If the answer is "Yes," you probably don't have a sale. If the answer is anything else, you have opened up the potential for discussion.

"THIS IS ALL VERY INTERESTING," a grizzled insurance sales veteran remarked in one of my workshops, "but you can't teach an old dog new tricks."

"That's too bad," I replied. "Most old dogs I know smell bad, can't see, their legs are gone, and they leave messes on the rug. They're completely dependent on their owner's love for survival. How loving are your owners?"

In a changing world, the alternative to growth and evolution is extinction. The good news is that we're all natural learners. It's part of the hard-wiring, even if we haven't used it a lot. It helps to think about learning the way Stephen Covey talks about loving.

> At one seminar where I was speaking on the concept of proactivity, a man came up and said, "Stephen, I like what you're saying. But every situation is so different. Look at my marriage. I'm really worried. My wife and I just don't have the same feelings for each other we used to have. I guess I just don't love her anymore and she doesn't love me. What can I do?"
> "Love her," I replied.
> "I told you, the feeling isn't there any more."
> "Love her."
> "You don't understand. The feeling of love just isn't there."
> "Then love her. If the feeling isn't there, that's a good reason to love her."
> "But how do you love when you don't love?"
> "My friend, love is a verb. Love—the feeling—is a fruit of love, the verb. So love her. Serve her. Sacrifice. Listen to her. Empathize. Appreciate. Affirm her."

Learning, like love, is something we have to do in order to enjoy. The action precedes the benefit. If you're concerned about failure, it's O.K. to practice new behaviors in relatively safe situations, small steps at a time, so long as you don't worry about outcomes, and pay attention instead to what is happening that is new and creative in your relationships. The Tao says, "The journey of a thousand miles begins with a single step." Then another. Then another. Tim Gallwey, in *Inner Skiing*, describes the process:

> My aim is to experience my skiing fully, to be as conscious as possible of body movements, skis, snow, rhythm, and balance. If I have a breakthrough run, I enjoy it, but I neither expect that I will ski that well on the next run, nor that I won't. Similarly, if I have a run which I know is less than my best, I don't form a judgment about myself or my skiing; I allow the past to stay in the past and leave the future open.... The point of the discovery game is not to find out how good you are, but to experience your potential as it continues to reveal itself.

Service

Quiet submissiveness is the strongest power in the world. It acts like
warming sunlight piercing to the center of a dense, hard stone, or
winter's cold splitting that same stone in pieces.

———————

ONE OF MY CLIENTS TOLD ME A STORY that captured for him what service
excellence in today's world is all about. He got a call from a long-standing client
one morning about an ongoing service problem they'd been struggling with.
"Let me tell you about my morning," she said. "I got in early, and decided to
get a little personal work done. So I called L.L. Bean about some birthday presents I wanted to order. The phone was answered immediately, and when I gave
the woman my name, there was a slight pause—I could hear the click of com-
puter keys—and then she said, 'Yes, Mrs. Wilson, thanks for calling us again. I
noticed that you bought some ski jackets and anoraks at Christmas. How did
they work out for you?' I told the salesperson my family was delighted with the
gifts. Then she asked, 'How can I help you today?' I placed a big order and felt
great about it.

"Next, I decided to check on a critical Federal Express shipment my department had to get to one of our customers. Same thing. I was recognized by name,
greeted warmly, and the account person had all the information I needed right at
his finger tips.

"Then I called you. Your new automatic phone system took me through a
maze of options I wasn't interested in. By the time I got to my fifth choice, I
couldn't remember the first two. All I wanted to do was speak to someone who
would help me with my problem. When, after the second call, I finally got a 'live
person,' I was put on hold while the 'Customer Support Liaison' tried to figure
out how to route the call. You weren't in yet, and he didn't have a clue about who
else could help. He finally suggested I call back later when 'somebody who is able
to help will be available,' thus forcing me to battle with your phone system again.
Get the point? You're not just in competition with your immediate competitors
for my business; you're competing with all the companies and people out there
who have made the decision to really offer service to customers."

To understand the power of submissiveness, it may help to consider that in
providing service to customers we are yielding not to the other person's demands,
but to the opportunities of that moment. This kind of surrender, therefore, does
not mean a loss of self-esteem but rather an increase of self-possession. We can
learn how we need to act from our customers.

 *Call your top customers this week and ask them to rate the
quality of the service you offer them.*

Where is the goodness in what you do?

Is it in your outward reputation or your inner self-knowledge?

Is it in your possessions or your self-possession? In the regard of others
or in your own self-esteem?

Gain or loss—which hurts more?

Be in graceful possession of yourself and you have that which cannot
be taken away.

There is no disgrace in contentment, no danger in being quiet and
calm, no loss when you seek nothing outside yourself.

PEOPLE SOMETIMES CONFUSE "SERVICE" with "servitude" and "servility." It's
easy to do that since these words all come from the same Latin root, *servus,* a slave.
Salespeople who feel the need to control situations or people often rebel against
being considered a "servant" of their customers—especially those customers
whose own needs for control lead to domineering behavior.

What are we being asked to let go of? To surrender?

- The need to be "right."
- The urge to dominate.
- The desire to control others.
- The fear that we may be "wrong."
- The fear that we may not live up to others' expectations.
- The fear that we don't really know much about where we're going.
- The fear that we may not be "smart" enough or "tough" enough
  to succeed.

"Surrendering" is weakness only if we view domination, manipulation, and
force as true strength. "Not Surrendering" is how we justify our own doubts
and lack of self-confidence. If we are truly powerful, we are free to act in each
situation simply and appropriately.

Excellent service is rooted in strong self-regard, and calm self-possession.

It is nourished through empathy and concern for customers' real well-
being.

It grows in the direction of real value: what's the best we can accomplish
together?

德 *Think of a client that you're not serving as completely as possible. Ask yourself, "What in me keeps me from going the whole
way with them?" Once you know, give what's needed.*

45. CONTRADICTION AND CONSISTENCY

Things are not always what they seem. The best advice often sounds
simple, even simple-minded, until it's put in practice. Actions
taken in someone else's behalf appear incomplete, even
contradictory in the doing, but complete themselves over time.

"Help me!"   ⇨   "How can you help yourself?"
"What should I do now?"   ⇨   "What do you want to do now?"

EXCELLENT SERVICE IS A PARADOX: strong assertiveness and total support at
the same time. That apparent contradiction may be confusing to customers.

Looking merely at what we do, customers and clients may become confused
or critical. "But you aren't doing anything!" "But that's so simple. Isn't there
something else we should do?" "Don't you have more to say about this?" "But I
was looking for an expert to tell me what to do!" "Aren't you going to give me
any answers?"

If we're really serving clients, it doesn't matter that we may initially
appear ignorant or unhelpful. Nor does it matter that our actions may, at
times, appear contradictory to them. Those feelings are in them, not in us. Their
confusion can be healthy. At the root of the word *confusion* is a sense of coming
together, of things merging.

The answer to their confusion is our consistency of purpose, demonstrated
in actions, not words. Those actions are characterized by the acronym "RATER."

Responsiveness: "Being there" for customers; taking all their
requests for service seriously; working with their sense of urgency
and concern about outcomes.

Authenticity: "Being real" with customers; communicating clearly
and openly, especially when difficult issues need to be resolved;
saying what you're going to do; doing what you say.

Tangible Results: Living with real outcomes as the measure of
success; no excuses, no blame.

Empathy: Getting out of your world and into the customers' world;
respecting how they view or understand things as legitimate for
them; customizing service for each customer.

Resourcefulness: Developing the full range of resources needed to
help customers achieve their goals; being a source of creativity,
imagination, and accomplishment.

德 *Create your own behavioral code of conduct based on the "RATER"
categories. Even better, show this list to a client and ask the client to
fill out how **he or she** would like **you** to act.*

46. INTERNAL CONTRACTING

When people treat each other in thoughtful, caring ways, no rules are
needed to enforce their friendship. When that thoughtful caring is
absent, the most expertly-drawn contract serves only to mark the
battlefield over which lawyers will fight—and prosper.

———————

THE REAL CONTRACTS YOU ESTABLISH with customers deal with the good faith
upon which the service relationship will be based. Those "contracts" involve your
entire organization.

I worked some years ago with a home medical supply company that was
rapidly expanding into new territories—and meeting stiff competition on price
from the established service provider. I went on a sales call with their best rep,
whose revenues were easily double those of the next best salesperson. We called
on a hospital who already had a long relationship with the competition. Instead
of arguing about who was better, his company or the competition, he affirmed
that what really mattered to the hospital was having the right medical support
equipment at the patient's home when the patient arrived back from the hospital. Then the rep asked, "How would you feel about a company that would have
the equipment there within an hour of your placing the order?"

"Great," responded the buyer, "but nobody can make good on that kind of
promise. Reality is getting it there the same day." "Then why not give me a
chance to improve on reality?" asked the rep. "Let me have your next order." At
the end of an hour, the van with the equipment was at the patient's home with a
trained medical technician to explain its use, waiting for the ambulance, patient,
and family to arrive. The rep got the business.

When I returned to the office, I noticed that this rep, unlike all the others,
walked in through the back, not the front. Before going to his desk, he chatted
with the drivers and planners, and asked how he could make their job easier,
strengthening the network that allowed him to transform "reality" into excellent
service.

No promise you make a customer is any better than the people in your organization responsible for carrying it out. Share the responsibility for success with
them. They are part of your team.

德 *Identify the people in your organization whose cooperation you
rely on to get the job done. Spend some time with them today
learning about what their problems are and how you can better serve them.*

Why travel all over the world looking for happiness when it is already waiting patiently within you?

The Tao says :

Without going outside, you may know the whole world. Without looking through the window, you may see the ways of heaven.

GIA-FU FENG AND JANE ENGLISH

In seeking knowledge and power, the further you travel from the wisdom inside you, the less you know and the weaker you become.

Truly wise and powerful people know that wisdom and power are gifts residing in them. No need therefore to look elsewhere for them.

Truly enlightened people understand the folly of looking to someone else for enlightenment.

Truly effective people accomplish what needs to be done without seeming to "do" anything.

OUR DESIRE TO KNOW MORE is driven by our fears of inadequacy. "If only I can understand more, read that book, master that formula for success, then I'll be able to cope with the world." But of course the complexity of the problems we wrestle with outruns the advice we receive. Just when we think we understand something, it changes on us. No amount of effort brings us the peace we seek.

Therefore, stop trying—start being.

"Being" begins with awareness. Are you fully conscious when you are with customers, free from the "noise" of your own concerns and desires? Regardless of your past history, are you alert to what is "new" about the customer in this moment?

"Being" is nurtured by trust. Do you trust yourself enough to find the thoughts and actions you need, when you need them, instead of trying to control the situation? Do you trust what you're selling enough to believe that it represents the right buying decision for the right customer?

"Being" is supported by commitment. Are you willing to live by the promises you make to the customer?

德 *Before your next sales call, ask yourself: "How can I deepen my awareness of what is happening between the customer and me? How can I strengthen my willingness to trust myself to work with the customer and the situation instead of trying to control things? What promises can I make that I will keep?"*

When we seek to become intelligent, knowledgeable "experts," we work each day to increase our store of information.

If we seek to become wise, we try each day to forget a little more of what we have learned.

If we let ourselves forget what we have learned, where does that knowledge go? It is deep inside us, ready to be used when we need it.

If our mind is free from knowledge, what does it possess? A greater awareness of what is happening right now. A greater capacity to act or not act, as the situation requires. Less force. More power.

What we call "knowledge" and "expertise" consists merely of the lessons of the past which may apply to the opportunities and challenges of the present moment, or may not.

––––––––––

NOTICE HOW PEOPLE AND COMPANIES trap themselves in knowledge. "This worked in the past. It should work now." "The trend has always been up. Therefore we'll bet the company's future that it will continue to rise." "Customers have always wanted this in the past. It must be what they want now." "We know who we are, and don't need to change."

Knowledge and expertise are appealing, especially in a changing, uncertain world, because they offer the illusion of security. They are also the greatest danger. What map do you follow in a strange, unexplored country?

Salespeople trap their customers and prospects in knowledge too. "My job is to 'educate' the customer on our products." While there is certainly value in providing information to customers that matches their needs and potential opportunities, more often than not, "education" takes the form of a canned speech or slide show—exactly the kind of non-learning that bored many of us to tears in school.

德 *In your next sales call, allow yourself to say whatever seems appropriate, but concentrate on allowing your breathing to become slow, deep, and natural. As you breathe in, "say" with part of your mind: "Everything I need will come to me." As you exhale, "say" to yourself "Everything that comes is a gift to share with this other person." Remember to smile as you breathe.*

*Resist the impulse to speak as soon as you have something to say. Speak only when something to say **has you.***

49. BEING "GOOD" TO PEOPLE

What we call "good" and "bad" is often our attempt to force our view of the world on other people. In truth, we are all staring at that part of the world we can see with our hands covering our eyes. That small part we dimly see we call "everything," and then divide it up into "good" and "bad."

What happens when we let go of "good" and "bad," "right" and "wrong"? We find that there is less bad in the world than we thought and more good, more that is in its own way "right," and less that is in our way "wrong."

———

I am kind to people when they are kind to me.
I am kind to them even if they hate me.
Virtue—te—is its own reward.
I trust those who trust me,
I also trust those who have no faith in me:
What I give, I receive.

MAN-HO KWOK,
MARTIN PALMER, JACK RAMSAY

IF YOU WISH TO TEST THIS, treat the customers you don't like the same as you treat those whom you do like, and see what happens. Treat the people whose actions you disapprove of the same way you treat the people whose actions you admire, and notice their response.

It helps if you expect less of the people you admire and merely give them space to be themselves. It helps if you allow the same space for the people you dislike.

德 *Ask someone to observe you when you make your next phone call to a client you really enjoy working with. Ask your "coach" to pay attention to your tone of voice, body posture, rate of breathing, skin color, and overall body "expression." Then have your coach observe you when you're talking to someone you don't get along with. Listen to the feedback from your coach with an open mind.*

Practicing:
SERVICE

1.   Start with value

What do you offer your customers or clients that is absolutely unique? If your initial answer is "nothing," then think some more. If you aren't unique, you're ordinary, and the lowest-priced competitor offering comparable ordinary service will get the business. Hint: Your uniqueness comes from your values—what you care about passionately or deeply. Try completing the following questions without thinking. Clear your mind, say the following statements to yourself, one at a time, and listen to the words that pop into your brain. Write them down immediately. They come from the Tao.

- The greatest value I bring people is my desire to....
- What I care most about in my life is....

2.   Define that value in concrete language

Write the answer to the above question on a piece of paper. Then take each key word and make it tangible. What does the idea look like, sound like, and feel like? Picture yourself **doing** these ideas with customers or clients. Hear the conversation. Experience the emotions. What is your uniqueness like when it happens with customers?

If, for example, your value to customers includes words like "trust," "loyalty," "accountability," or "creativity," then ask yourself: "How do I **do** trust?" "How do I **do** loyalty?" Keep asking until you have concrete descriptions of specific actions that distinguish you from others in the same business as you.

3.   Translate that value into the customer's world

What will customers get from the unique value you offer that will increase the value of **their** business, **their** lives, or **both**? Notice we're not talking about products or services, we're talking about you. How does the experience of working with you enable customers or clients to do more, have more, or be more? If at this stage you're talking about what your products and services do, then you're answering the wrong question. What happens in the customers' world when they use what you offer?

> *Ted Averbook is a highly successful mutual funds salesperson working for CMG in Canada. He defines his value to the investment clients he serves very simply: "I help my clients sleep at night, knowing they've make a smart, appropriate investment decision for their future. My value is that I help clients lower their anxiety level about how their money is invested so they can do other things they care about."*

4.   Communicate that value to your clients

Be clear about what you value and the value you offer. Practice stating your deepest, most powerful convictions until you can say them, in a sentence or two, to every new client or prospect, with complete confidence and integrity. Completing any of the statements below will help you communicate the value you offer clients. Say the words below and then listen to your mind as it completes the thought. Write down what your mind gives you, then refine the statement until it has clarity, conviction, and complete integrity.

- "Any time we work together, you can count on me to...."
- "The most important thing to me in my client relationships is that...."
- "As a salesperson, I believe that...."

5.   Translate your values into a code of conduct

Think about all the situations that might cause you to waver or stumble in keeping the value-based promises you make to customers. Chances are money will have a lot to do with those challenges. "I'd live up to my values if I just had a little more steady business." "I'd practice what I believe in if I didn't need this sale." Think through the long and short-range consequences of not offering value to customers. Make a choice. Live with the consequences.

6.   Increase that value

Ask yourself: "How can I do what I value more completely, more simply, more enthusiastically?" "How can I turn my uniqueness into a bright light that attracts customers to me?" The myth of selling is that we have to constantly hustle to get business, knocking on doors, making demeaning (and irritating) cold calls, "pitching our wares." Notice that when you do that, you become just like everybody else again. If you run ads, everybody runs ads. If you make cold calls, everybody makes cold calls (and most of them are annoying, unconscious, and pushy)—that's whom you've lumped yourself together with. If, on the other hand, you consistently add value in your dealings with clients, they will become a value-added network for you.

7.   Share the value

One key to excellent service is resourcefulness, the ability to have the resources to meet customer's complex, specialized needs. You develop these resources by earning them—sharing your knowledge and expertise with people whose businesses overlap or support yours, in partnership. How to develop these relationships? Offer others the same value you offer customers. How to maximize these relationships? Give with no strings attached to people who share comparable values.

PR NEWSWIRE IS AN INFORMATION services company that has grown from its roots in financial wire services to become the leading electronic distributor of full text corporate news to the media and financial community world-wide, through the newswire, fax, bulletin board systems, and the Internet.

In November, 1993, they initiated a total organizational commitment to becoming a "service champion," gaining market share and generating profits through the quality of the service they offered clients. That commitment included major investments in new client-servicing technology and people resources, backed by major training initiatives.

That commitment was severely tested a year later, in the early fall of 1994, when PR Newswire's major competitor launched an all-out price war spearheaded by deep discounting offers to their client base. PR Newswire's salespeople started calling in with reports of competitive discounts of as much as 50 percent off the basic fees paid by their existing clients, for what their competition assured their clients would be "fully comparable service." In a climate of cost-cutting, in which clients were looking to stretch cost dollars to the maximum, the danger to PR Newswire was serious, and urgent. Their most loyal clients were calling them saying, "I want to keep working with you, and appreciate all you do for us, but I'm responsible to my boss. How can I turn down a price break like this and still say I'm doing the best for my company? You have to help me out. What can you do about lowering your price?"

When I met with PR Newswire's Executive Committee, the issues were clear. They had to mount a strong response, one that would meet the challenges being presented by both their competition and their clients. Trying merely to "protect" accounts on a case-by-case basis wouldn't work; once they started cutting prices to keep business, the downward slide would accelerate, "case-by-case." Because of their investment in people and resources to meet client needs, severe price cuts would attack not only the profits they were required to achieve, but also their fundamental service capacity. In a highly-competitive business, however, the loss of even a few major accounts in key industries could start an equally damaging downward slide that their competition was poised to exploit.

Their salesforce, battling in the trenches against fierce price pressure, needed immediate direction and support. No salesperson likes to lose a major account. To lose good business that you've cultivated for years, simply because the competition was willing to buy it more cheaply than your company could afford, was galling, frustrating, even scary.

Their response was bold, and courageous. They decided to fight it out at the level of value to their customers, in effect, turning a price war into a choice for quality service. "We looked at our assets as a company," recalled CEO Ian Capps. "They included the quality of our people, our willingness to trust our service commitment, and the investment we'd made in technical systems that allowed us to customize products and services to meet clients' immediate and future needs. We had to meet the challenge with our best strengths, and not get pulled into a war of attrition that negated those strengths."

The Executive Committee agreed on the need to hold firm to their strategy. "I don't want to see us lose a single client," stressed John Williams, Executive VP of Sales. "Every single client is important. We've got to be smart enough not only to fight this battle, but win it. But if push comes to shove, and the price of keeping a client is sacrificing what we believe in, then we have to be tough enough to say 'no' to that demand."

That week they initiated a "discounting counter-attack," triggered by a clear policy statement to all bureaus stating the company's position clearly and firmly. Within two weeks they launched a nation-wide service workshop "blitz," region by region, that included:

- Frank discussion about the company's response and commitment to holding the line on price and value-added service.

- A specific response to client "bottom line" concerns, that put real dollar amounts on what clients had taken for granted in value-added service. ("Here's what you get from us now for free. If you buy cut rate you won't be getting those services any more. What does it cost you to do without them? Suppose you had to purchase them on the open market?")

- Training in the economics of their business that allowed salespeople to point out the value to their clients of PR Newswire's investment in technological resources. ("When you needed to add Fax-On-Demand to meet your customer's needs, we were already set up for you. Suppose you'd had to wait six months for us or the competition to develop the capacity? Part of what we charge is reinvested in the capacity to be there for you when you need us.")

- Training in turning the apparent advantage of the competitor's lower price into an actual disadvantage to the customer. ("If they attack their own profits so drastically, how long do you think they can afford to charge this price?" "What happens to the service you receive when they've cut back to the bone?")

- Training in targeted appeals to the customer's best interests. ("You're trying to expand the quality service you can offer your clients. What happens to that quality if the people you rely on can't afford to expand with you?")

- Selling the value of partnership with PR Newswire as the best way for clients to meet their own long-term growth needs.

- Specific linkage between expanded service or volume and price relief. ("If you increase business with us, that reduces our cost of sales; we'll happily return that cost-savings to you in reduced rates.")

Over the following months, the initial blitz was supported, internally, by stronger coordination within internal systems and between the sales force and internal customer support. It was backed up by accelerated and expanded use of Lotus Notes as a company-wide data base available to everyone who worked with clients, including systems support and client billing. Client service became everybody's job.

Ironically, one of the greatest benefits of the competitive price war was that it forced the company to look at all its internal systems, including service and billing, to make sure they supported the company-wide commitment to service.

In the first year, the results were positive and dramatic. In addition to holding off the attack, they started taking clients away from the competition. One example tells the story. The Cleveland Bureau received a call from a long-standing customer, reporting the competitive offer, of a 40 percent discount over three years. At the time they were doing $15,000 a year, roughly one third of the client's total budget. By the time the meeting was over, they had added international wire services to help the client speed up its international expansion, plus web service, Fax-On-Demand to better communicate with shareholders, internal fax services to communicate better within the company, and photo wire service to support their stories with the media.

PRN invested time and resources with the client by providing training for the staff to improve their internal communication with PRN and helped the client work with key media to improve the quality and value of their stories. By the time they were done, what had been a good relationship at a small-scale level had grown into a strategic partnership. Revenues with this client are now in the $100,000 range, with a cost-value balance that works for both the client and PRN.

One year-and-a-half after the initial attack, PR Newswire's client base, market share, and profits have never been stronger, and they've exceeded projected revenues.

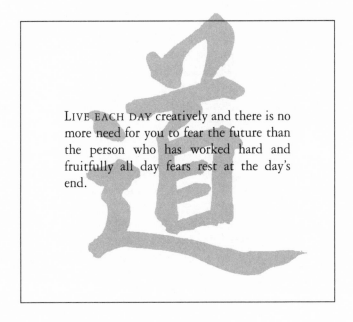

LIVE EACH DAY creatively and there is no more need for you to fear the future than the person who has worked hard and fruitfully all day fears rest at the day's end.

Creating

Some people spend their lives in fear of death, constantly seeking to avoid the inevitable. Some people spend their lives in fear of life, constantly missing the joy of what is possible.

Some people enjoy life while alive and don't fear death because until it happens they are still alive. Plenty of time to cope with death when we're dead.

Whatever we fear is waiting around the next corner each day of our journey through life. The less we fear, the more open and untroubled that road.

On your best, your happiest day, did you think about anything at all, or did you just experience that day in its fullness? Where was time then? Where was worry?

———

CREATIVITY IS THE CAPACITY TO BRING to life something that has only existed before in potentiality. In a global marketplace of rapid, unsettling change, scarce resources, and unpredictable competitive challenges, customers and clients need creative solutions more than ever.

What stops creativity dead in its tracks is fear: "What if this doesn't work?" "Suppose I get different results from what I anticipated?" "What if something goes wrong?" "Suppose I get blamed?" Fear can cause us to choose the illusory safety and comfort of a slow death over the exhilaration of creative, on-going life.

Being a creative resource for our customers starts with releasing the hold of our own fear. Thich Nhat Hanh, in *Peace is Every Step*, teaches the loving discipline of treating our fears as if they were a hurt, crying child within us. We would want to hear the child, not ignore it; comfort it, not become angry at its pain; and then help it understand what scared it, so the power of the fear can go away.

If you say "But I'm not creative," remember that creativity is a gift of the Tao, or God, in whatever way you worship or understand spirit to operate in the world. By opening up to that creative spirit, you get all the "creativity" you need.

德 *Make a list on a piece of paper or in your journal of any fears or beliefs you may have about your lack of creativity. Look for creative ways to move beyond those fears.*

If you say "I don't know how to be creative," remember that for the past 500 years, people have raised an artificial barrier, called "reason," against natural creativity. "Reason" was turned into a golden idol to be worshiped in the name of Control, Certainty, and Conquest. So "profit," "bottom line," "results now," "logical analysis," and "practicality" became virtues, and anything which appeared to oppose those "virtues" became, automatically, "wrong."

That barrier has had the effect of dividing not only the brain but the mind against itself. But all of us are born with both a "left," rational brain and a "right," creative brain. Otherwise we'd be running around like half-wits. The capacity is there in all of us, because it is there in the entire created universe. No need to search it out or struggle to find it. It's as available as the air we breathe.

GEOFF PRICE RUNS HIS OWN MICRO-BREWERY and pub in Long Valley, NJ, but when he started working in 1973, operating a brewery was the furthest thing from his mind. After getting a degree in mechanical engineering, he started working for a small combustion engineering firm in Stamford, CT, and for seventeen years grew with the company to a position of pride and responsibility, working as an internal systems consultant. Then the mergers started. By the second time the company had been acquired and merged, he was a cog in a very large machine, wondering "Is this what I gave all those years to? Is this what it was all about?"

Long Valley, where Geoff lives, is a quiet, historical town. Over the years, on his trips to the airport, Geoff would drive by a large stone barn, built in 1771, that was now abandoned, sitting in a messy lot full of weeds. As he passed the barn he would think, "Wouldn't it be great if someone fixed up that wonderful old building and found a new use for it before it falls down and is lost forever?" In some ways, it was as if the barn were just waiting for him.

Geoff adds, "During those ten or fifteen years as a consultant, I gained a lot of experience traveling to different places and talking to a lot of people, seeing what happens in the rest of the U.S. I visited the West Coast a lot, and watched the growth of micro-breweries and brew pubs springing up out there during the late '80s.

"I found myself thinking and dreaming about my childhood in the U.K. Pubs are a way of life there. They're part of the community. One of my old aunts tells me my great-great-great-uncle used to deliver and make beer back in the 1700s. So there's a little bit of that in my history. And I thought, why not run a brew pub that kind of gets back to my roots?"

Those thoughts merged with his dissatisfaction with his career into the decision to build a micro-brewery and restaurant in the barn, using his engineering experience to complete the construction phase and then learn the restaurant business step-by-step. One of his first moves was to realize that this could be a community effort. So he enlisted the support of town government, local businesses, and residents to use the brew pub as a center for the town.

"The place has become a destination now. People came to this area before for the pumpkin picking and those types of family activities, but now they can come out and do that pumpkin picking and know they have a few restaurants in town to come to and eat. That means that the local village association, which is just a bunch of us baker's men, we gather and we strap the jive on about how we can keep these people in town when they come."

His second creative breakthrough was to realize that his "audience" of customers and resources was the entire country. "By talking with other micro-brewery owners, I got ideas and tips from all over the U.S. People were happy to help. It's incredible the number of people that knew we were coming and waited patiently for us. There's like a subculture of beer geeks that get on the Internet; they're highly technical people and they communicate about where these brew pubs are and we get people from Bergen county, from Pennsylvania, down in Cape May, which is south New Jersey."

The third creative breakthrough was to stage not a restaurant opening, but a town-wide festival. A year before he opened, in 1994, Long Valley held its first Oktoberfest. In large part because of Internet advertising and word of mouth, almost 20,000 people showed up. The second year, in time for his opening, over 25,000 people attended. Not bad for a restaurant launch.

"Part of the thrill was transforming an old, decaying stone barn into a vibrant brew pub with a great deal of ambiance. We kept the lofty roof and we made a balcony on the second floor and we kept the basic material in the design, stone, some wrought iron, and some wonderful woodworking. So it's very gratifying to see this project come to fruition and other people coming in to enjoy the place. I just love going down there to watch people come in the door and just look around and say 'Wow!' And business is great."

德 *Spend the next week becoming more open to the "answers" to the questions you are grappling with, that are hanging there, like ripe fruit.*

51. ACTING NATURALLY

Everything is created by the Tao of Nature
—and from everything on earth that surrounds it.

MAN-HO KWOK, MARTIN PALMER, JACK RAMSAY

Look at a field in winter. Brown stalks crack in the cold. Dried, brittle leaves scrape across the wind-driven frozen ground. See the same field in spring. Daffodils stretch to greet the sun and birds celebrate the earth's re-awakening.

Your grandparents, looking at the same field, would have seen no less. So will your grandchildren, unless, in our carelessness, we have allowed the field to be covered over in concrete.

What might it mean to act naturally?

When we accept that we are merely part of nature, we allow ourselves to be nourished, created, cared for, comforted in our time, and then taken back into that from which we sprung. Neither possessed nor possessing, guided but not controlled, sheltered but not enclosed, enjoying without expectation.

WHEN WE ACCEPT THE EMPTINESS of ego and fullness of spirit that links us with all creation we become more open to creativity.
- Let go of all "should"s and "shouldn't"s; the plant does not ask permission to bloom.
- Let go of all comparisons; the sun does not run beauty contests among the flowers.
- Let go of urgency about "how"; the river doesn't have to do a "time and motion study" to run downhill.
- Accept the effortless power given to you. Trees lift tons of water forty feet high in the air each day with no effort; that energy explodes into showers of green that create the air we breathe. They need no "re-engineering."

Creativity is a "whole earth/whole brain" process—seeing things in relation to the whole. It means living easily with the apparent clutter and complexity of it all—the "good" and the "bad," the "beautiful" and the "ugly," the "safe" and the "scary," all together. We start by realizing that customers are part of the solution, no matter how they appear to oppose or thwart us.

德 *Take a current situation or challenge you are confronting and view it from the different perspectives of all the people involved: "From their perspective, they see the issue as...." Put the core issue in the center of a piece of paper and write all the varying points of view around the center. That's the real problem. That's where the solution will come from.*

A miracle is never lost. It may touch many people you have not even met, and produce undreamed of changes in situations of which you are not even aware.... The Holy Spirit's Voice is as loud as your willingness to listen.

A COURSE IN MIRACLES

Each day reminds us that we are mortal—that things rise into being and die and are born anew. Each of us has the time we have been given to grow, blossom, fade, and die.

When did the seed from which you came into the world first get sown? What is your real beginning? What do you know of your real roots in the generations of time? For what unknown children, in unknowable future times, are you now the seed? The action you took today—when does it cease echoing throughout the universe?

———

John Hone has run a successful painting business for eighteen years, through fat and lean years in the economy. As a company committed to excellent quality and outstanding service, he's always under "attack" from house painters willing to work for much less. In building a quality service reputation, he has recognized that the work he turns down is as important as the customers he agrees to work for. "When I cut my price just to get the business, I cut my quality, and thus kill my business. For me, creativity is being able to balance both profit, which we need, and great service, which we also need. People want to look at a paint job years after it's been done and feel good about choosing us as a painter. Sometimes the best decision we make is saying 'no,' letting the customer choose another painter that works 'cheap,' and then finally having them come back to us to get it done right."

ALL OUR ACTIONS WITH CUSTOMERS and colleagues are significant—all are seeds—none are insignificant. The gardener does not know, beforehand, which seeds will bloom into lush, fruitful plants. The ground we plant these seeds in is the trust that exists between us and others. The seeds have names: "Compassion," "Openness," "Integrity," "Patience." There are weeds in the garden too. Their names include "Anger," "Suspicion," "Self-doubt," and "Urgency." How does your garden grow?

德 *This simple truth has an equally simple, practical application. Imagine, each time you are with a customer, that you are merely planting new seeds and nourishing those that have already blossomed, with the same patient, loving care of the master gardener. The harvest will come in its time.*

Following the truth is easy. Ignoring the truth, fighting against it—
that's really hard.

Because truth is planted deeply within us, all we need to do to stay
balanced is to pay attention to the nature of things.

All we need to do to understand imbalance is to look at the world that
people create in the effort to control things.

> *When the court is arrayed in splendor,*
> *The fields are full of weeds,*
> *And the granaries are bare.*
> *Some wear gorgeous clothes,*
> *Carry sharp swords,*
> *And indulge themselves with food and drink;*
> *They have more possessions than they can use.*
> *They are robber barons.*
> *This is certainly not the way of the Tao.*
>
> GIA-FU FENG AND JANE ENGLISH

True creativity always serves the purposes of the Creator. That's why
we can surrender to it.

———

IN RECENT YEARS SCIENTISTS HAVE LEARNED a tremendous amount about the
workings of the brain; we still know almost nothing about the mind, and can't
even say for sure where it's located.

The whole problem with Western civilization is that ever since the Greeks we've been
trying to squeeze the mind into the brain—and it won't fit.

MEL ZIEGLER

The part of our mind we use to create is the part we share with all creation. Many
studies of creative people in every field throughout history confirm that. Clearly
the breakthrough thoughts that enter our consciousness come from somewhere.
But where? We don't control the creative process, but we can share in it.

德 *Think for a moment about a complex problem confronting your*
organization. What kinds of efforts have been made to "fix" the
problem? What kinds of results have you experienced?

CLEVER PEOPLE COME UP with good solutions; wise people come up with good questions.

The useful creative questions are not "How can we make things happen?" "How can we solve this problem?" "How do we improve this situation?" When we approach situations in this way, we automatically (and unconsciously) trigger all the assumptions of the past, all the "rights and wrongs" built over the years into our belief systems, and start looking at things through the "blinders" imposed by our desires and fears. The "solutions" which this process leads to tend to generate almost as many new problems as they were intended to solve in the first place.

> There is a profound difference between problem solving and creating. Problem solving is taking action to have something go away—the problem. Creating is taking action to have something come into being—the creation. The problem solvers propose elaborate schemes to define the problem, generate alternative solutions, and put the best solution into practice. If this process is successful, you might eliminate the problem. But what you do not have is the presence of a result you want to create.
>
> ROBERT FRITZ

THIS BECOMES CLEARER WHEN WE stop thinking of the world as a machine, and understand it to be a complex, interrelated, natural, living organism. Tinker with one part to "fix" it, and five other things change, three of which we didn't even include in the scope of the original "problem." Then those "problems" need to be "fixed," generating five more new, unanticipated "problems."

Think of the patient suffering from a complex disease. The patient is subjected to dozens of complicated tests which yield lots of data about what's wrong, but don't clearly indicate a cure. So the doctors (often specialists in a narrow area) throw the latest miracle drug at the symptom. The initial symptoms improve, but the body "resists" with new, sometimes more troubling, painful side effects. Treat those with more drugs, and unexpected adverse drug reactions set in. And, with each treatment, the virus "learns" a little more about how to defeat the drug. Meanwhile, back at the lab, the cost of trying to "outwit" nature with newer, more specialized drugs, escalates so much that fewer and fewer people can afford the "cure."

德 *How comfortable are you with uncertainty and ambiguity? Do you wait for the "right" answer, or withhold making your voice heard until there's a safe consensus? Do you push a decision just to make something happen? Think about decisions you have been avoiding. Pick one decision your "gut" has already chosen and act on it this week. Think about a decision you feel a lot of urgency to make, even though you suspect you're just "treating the symptoms." Ask five people to give you feedback about what you're missing in the situation.*

54. PUTTING DOWN ROOTS

The Tao—really, the truth of things—is like a deeply rooted tree. Strong winds beat upon it and it stands firm amidst the gales.

Embrace the Tao and your own roots will reach deep and strong into the nourishing earth. Ignore it, and each changing wind, however slight, can uproot you.

Let it flourish inside you and you will truly know peace. Plant it within your family and the people you love will grow and flower. Nourish it within your community and wise leaders will arise as they are needed. Speak truth and the entire universe will sing with you. How do you know this is true? Listen to the song within you.

––––––––

THE REAL "BOTTOM LINE" PAYOFF for developing trust-based relationships with clients is the enormous potential you gain in encouraging their own creativity, resourcefulness, and commitment. Even better, when your creativity works with theirs, you have the opportunity for breakthrough thinking and genuine synergy. It's exactly the same with colleagues. Trust is the fertile soil in which success grows.

德 *Planting instructions:*
When the impatience inside of you says, "Listen to me!" be quiet. Listen to what the other person is saying.

When the self-doubt inside you says, "BUT WHAT ABOUT MY IDEA!" be quiet. Then explore the other person's idea.

When the intolerance inside you or others says, "THAT'S THE WRONG WAY!" be quiet. Once you understand the other person's idea, ask how you can put it together creatively with what you believe.

When the urgency inside you or others says, "BUT WE NEED A SOLUTION NOW!" remember the frustration, duplication of effort, and missed opportunity that happened the last time a premature solution was forced into place. A better question is, "What can we do, now, while we still work on an eventual solution?"

When the fear inside you or others says, "BUT THAT WILL NEVER WORK! THEY'LL NEVER BUY THAT!" treat the resistance as an opportunity. "How can we work with them to gain their acceptance?"

Creativity happens best in a relaxed, even playful interaction with others when we suspend the urgent demands of ego and the need to compete.

Think of yourself when you were an infant. What fear was strong enough to keep you from walking? What insecurity kept you from talking? What knowledge kept you from experiencing each new sensation with wonder instead of judgment?

Fear, insecurity, judgment, bias, doubt, hatred, envy, jealousy—these are all learned. Growth, discovery, wonder, joy—these are all naturally within us from birth.

Masterful people are childlike. They allow the world to happen and allow themselves to experience it fully. They don't try to impose their will upon it and then become angry when the world refuses to obey. Because they expect nothing they are not disappointed. Because they anticipate nothing, they are not frustrated by events.

Living without desire, anger, disappointment, and frustration, the master's spirit stays forever young.

THE PLAYFUL QUESTIONS EMBRACE POSSIBILITY and open ourselves and others to discovery. "What would happen if...." "Suppose we tried...." "Let's imagine there were no obstacles and we were free to do what we want."

Because the power of the past is so strong a limit on the sense of discovery, creative thinking works best when it's not viewed as a way to "solve" current problems, but operates, instead, freely in the future. The easy way to accomplish creative thinking is to put yourself and the others you're working with deliberately and specifically in the future—two or three years away. (If you're thinking creatively about an organization, five or ten years is not too long a projection.)

德 *Imagine that within the time allotted, you have been able to design and implement the ideal reality you wish. If you were successful, that's what you would have done. Simply assume the success without, for the moment, worrying about the "how." Create a clear, vivid, detailed vision of that ideal future. What are you doing together, with what resources, in what ways, to accomplish what results? What does it feel like? What are you looking at? What are you hearing?*

Once the future design is clear and vivid, then work backward from the future to the present. What actions taken in year three, allowed you to complete the future design in year four? What did you do in year two, that made the accomplishments of year three possible? And so on until you reach the present. Then start doing what you already have done.

56. ACTING LIKE A CHILD

Infants have little to say; they are too busy learning and discovering. Adults have a lot to say about what they have learned and discovered; the more they talk, the less they learn and thus the less they know until finally they know nothing and can't learn anything new.

> *Close your mouth,*
> *block off your senses,*
> *blunt your sharpness,*
> *untie your knots,*
> *soften your glare,*
> *settle your dust.*
>
> STEPHEN MITCHELL

We can nourish the creativity within us through meditation and inner calm.

———————

CREATE A TIME IN THE DAY to give yourself the gift of peaceful reflection. Plan everything else around that time. God did not defer the creation of the world to attend a Board Meeting. You get "voice mail" from the Tao each day. Answer that call first. The other people can wait.

Thich Nhat Hanh suggests creating a "place of reflection" within the home. Whoever is sitting in that place has the right not to be interrupted; it's a right all people in the home need to honor and respect for themselves and all family members. It's a wonderful, healing refuge for people who need space to let go of anger. Remember not to chase them into the space and feed their anger. There are even corporations now that give the same gift to all employees, managers, and executives without exception.

德 *Enter a place of physical peacefulness, and allow the place of peacefulness inside you to grow. Sit in a way that is comfortable to you.*

 • *Close your mouth: Be quiet. Breathe through your nose, and feel the energy flow into you with each breath, filling your entire body. Allow that breath to fill you for four or five seconds. Exhale fully and completely, emptying yourself over four or five seconds. Many people find it helps to repeat a positive affirmation as they breathe in such as "I have all the love and wisdom I need." As they exhale, they share that energy in a second affirmation, such as "I can give this love and wisdom to the entire world."*

 • *Block off your senses: Release all physical feelings of tension, tightness, and even pain, each time you exhale, starting, if you wish, with the muscles of your face, head, and neck, and then gradually allowing peacefulness to fill your entire body.*

91

- *Blunt your sharpness: It is natural for thoughts to enter your mind, even troubling or anxious thoughts. Allow them to leave your mind effortlessly, without either attention or resistance.*

- *Untie your knots: Allow yourself to consider some issue you are wrestling with. Release all your conscious and unconscious desires regarding that issue, so that a creative response can come to you. Let go of all assumptions about "right" and "wrong," "possible" and "impossible." God did not run an opinion poll before creating humanity (thank goodness!).*

- *Soften your glare: Allow yourself to see the issue completely from the other person's perspective. Remember that "all human behavior is either an expression of love or a cry to be loved."*

- *Settle your dust: Release all feelings of past anger and hurt. No blame on either side, no accusations or guilt.*

From that place of peacefulness, go on a journey inside your mind. Take yourself to a place in your imagination that has peaceful, happy, whole memories for you. Let yourself walk in that remembered place, using as many of your senses as you can: sight, smell, hearing, taste, touch, and inner emotion. Imagine then that there is, in that place, a door you can approach. Let yourself experience the door in whatever detail you choose. When you are ready, open the door and walk through it without fear. You can trust whatever you find on the other side. Perhaps there is a person on the other side, someone real from your past, a historical personage, or someone you have discovered in your imagination. Imagine that the person waiting there has a healing, caring message for you. Allow yourself to take that message in completely, no matter what form it takes.

As you return to daily activities, reflect upon the meaning of the message until a course of action becomes clear.

In his translation of the *Tao Te Ching*, Stephen Mitchell includes a wonderful comment on all this by his teacher, Zen Master Seung Sahn:

> *Our mind is like a glass of clear water. If we put salt into the water, it becomes salt water; sugar, it becomes sugar water; shit, it becomes shit water. But originally the water is clear. No thinking, no mind. No mind, no problem.*

Practicing:
CREATING

1.   **Break routines**
Deliberately change routines in your life: how you drive to work, the repetitious pattern of daily responsibilities, the habitual activities in the evening (especially if they include "couch potato" absorption into the mindlessness of broadcast TV). When you do something "new," pay attention to everything you can learn about people, the world around you, and yourself. Enjoy the gift of discovery.

2.   **Challenge assumptions**
Identify an assumption or rule you currently operate by. Allow yourself to imagine what could happen, in a productive, creative way, if that assumption or rule were not true. Allow yourself to act, immediately, on any actions that come to you which you feel you could initiate in good conscience.

3.   **See things "whole"**
Go some place where the natural world is still relatively intact and complete: growing things, open sky, and water (ideally flowing) are essential ingredients. Find a growing plant or tree, and visualize its complete cycle through the seasons and over the reach of time: earth, seed to flower, and back to earth and seed. Follow the water from its source, to where you are, to the end of its journey, and back to the source. Imagine the water is a mirror. What images have appeared in that mirror? The mirror is flat and static. It makes no judgments. Meanwhile, the water within it keeps flowing. Discover the balance within the entire natural space, all things creating and sharing energy. If you're lucky, and natural animals (not pets) are part of the space, observe their contribution to the whole. Explore the connection between earth, plant, and sky. Allow time for all the sounds of the place to enter your awareness without categorizing or trying to separate them out. (In today's world of machines that may be tough; but the natural sounds are still there to be heard.) Breathe the entire space into yourself. Walk around the space and discover it from new perspectives. If you feel really bold, what the hell, hug a tree. Then remember that you are part of the same process, and act accordingly.

4.   **Simplify what appears complex; find the inherent pattern in "chaos"**
Most problems concerning people and processes have become extraordinarily complex by the time the pain they cause finally galvanizes someone to act on them. Dealing with the complexity may be too difficult. Within all complex problems are very simple patterns of meaning. Work with the simple pattern and the complex will "fix" itself.

   • "Solve" problems impacting hundreds of people by paying attention
     to what needs to happen between any two people who interact:

buyer and seller, customer and supplier, internal service department and internal clients, "boss" and "subordinate." If the interaction between any two people is healthy, productive, and purposeful, and if that's the way all people are encouraged to treat each other, two will add up to hundreds and thousands.

- "Solve" process problems by imagining the simplest, least-cluttered movement of energy from the start of the process to the end. For example, if there were no rules, procedures, departments, assumptions, past history, artificial boundaries, or protected "turf," what would be the easiest, simplest way to move from supply to production to delivery to payment? Think of it as a natural flow of energy, such as light, water, or electricity. Remove all the obstacles and barriers that create friction (and increase heat). Imagine that it's an expanding, growing circle or a spiral, such as: Satisfied customer ⇨ new inquiry ⇨ clarification of need ⇨ customization of resources ⇨ fulfillment ⇨ service support ⇨ satisfied customer ⇨ new inquiry…. How can you streamline the process so that it wastes as little internal energy as possible? ("Energy" means money, information, time, and physical effort.)

5. Develop creative discovery skills and share them with others
There are hundreds of books on how to think creatively. All these skills can be used with anyone you work with, most of them effortlessly. In most cases, all you need to do to apply these skills is ask permission and invite collaboration. "Suppose we brainstorm this?" "Suppose we look at this another way?" "It feels like we're all stuck on this issue. Why don't we approach it from a brand new perspective and see what we find?"

Remember that when you encounter resistance, the best response is a question, not a statement. "But how can we do this within our current budget?" "I don't know. How **can** we do this within our current budget?"

6. Learn to think "naturally"
If organizations are machines, control make sense. If organizations are process structures, then seeking to impose control through permanent structure is suicide … a treadmill of effort and life-destroying stress. What if we could reframe the search? What if we stopped looking for control and began, in earnest, the search for order? Order we will find in many places we never thought to look before—all around us in nature's living, dynamic systems that are open to their environment. In fact, once we begin to look into nature with new eyes, the examples are overwhelming.

MARGARET WHEATLEY

"Thinking naturally" can happen in metaphor or play. Both kinds of activities put us back in touch with the creative unconscious present in all of us, but often submerged beneath our fears and assumptions. Ted Coulson and Alison Strickland, of Applied Creativity, are just two of the hundreds of consultants out there who have helped business people in all areas find workable, breakthrough solutions through metaphor and "playfulness."

Their process includes these actions: — NICE ,

- Build a "It would be nice if…" list. Let yourself think "wishfully."

- Think and talk about what you want in place of what you have. Describe what you want in writing.

- Do a mind map of what you want. Explore new patterns of action and invite new connections.

- Mentally walk into the future. Imagine that the problem has been solved. Look around you. What's going on that tells you the "problem" has been "solved"?

- Develop a metaphor for what has happened. Compare what you are working with and wish to create to something else, and follow the possibilities first within the metaphor, then back into the real situation.

7.   **Welcome and work with fear of the unknown and uncertainty about outcomes.**

John Pehrson and Jeanne Borei of Creative Change Technologies, who run their own highly-successful creativity- and community-building workshops, call this extension beyond our comfort zone "the shadow." It happens as people move past the comfortable routines of thought and action into really unexplored territory. It is often experienced as "chaos"—the sense that once old, comforting rules are eliminated, and creative possibilities open up, that no rules or guidelines exist. The point is that this discomfort—or feeling "lost" or threatened—is a healthy part of the process; a necessary step on the way to creation.

Facing the shadow is an experience that challenges each of us to examine the core of our soul, to see the "stuff" of which we are made. It presents us with the opportunity to move through the quagmire of obstacles we find within us— feelings, belief systems, old baggage—to a new way of being. We have the opportunity to become people of true courage and deep integrity.

The application of all this to selling is clear. Creativity is both an innate gift we all enjoy and a set of learned skills and behaviors. The more mastery we gain in the creative process, the more value we bring customers, especially when we include them as partners in the creative act.

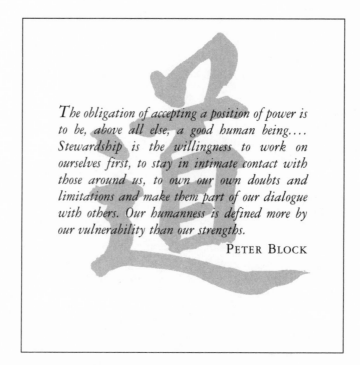

The obligation of accepting a position of power is to be, above all else, a good human being.... Stewardship is the willingness to work on ourselves first, to stay in intimate contact with those around us, to own our own doubts and limitations and make them part of our dialogue with others. Our humanness is defined more by our vulnerability than our strengths.

PETER BLOCK

Leading by Following

Who are the great leaders? Those who let go of the need to control everything and instead pay attention to how things are evolving.

If we believe the world (in its essence, apart from human "improvements") is fundamentally coherent, deeply rational, purposeful, and beautifully formed, then why not make our actions harmonious with that sense of order and flow?

Pay attention to the messages the world gives you:

The more rules you create, the more rules you need—to stop the clever people who excel at breaking them.

The more you try to defend yourself, the more you need to defend yourself, until the whole world is full of enemies.

The more you reward people for being good, the more you strip them of real integrity. The reward takes the place of the act.

———

IT IS HARD IN TODAY'S WORLD to be a sales manager, let alone a leader. Often we are smothered in data and starved for real knowledge, blown every which way by demands and rarely able to get through a day in which we feel a sense of accomplishment.

德 *Do you ask people for their loyalty and commitment? Or give orders? Learn to separate communication and command. Since you have the freedom to do whatever you believe is best, and the authority of your integrity to support that choice, there is nothing to fear in letting people express themselves fully.*

You have the right, as the leader of a group, to be clear about the values you want that group to live by (the same values, in fact, that you are willing to live by in your dealings with them). Offer them the choice of working as a community by those values. Allow them the tolerance of figuring out with you how that work will be done.

58. TOLERANCE AND REPRESSION

Govern with tolerance and the people will be relaxed and honest.
Govern by repression and people will react with selfishness,
cruelty, and greed.

How do we know this is true? By simple observation of others and
attention to our own feelings.

———————

If you govern with a generous hand—
then your people will be good people.
But if your system is too constricting
then your people will outwit you. . .

MAN-HO KWOK,
MARTIN PALMER, JACK RAMSAY

THE EXCUSE FOR REPRESSION is the belief that people need to be controlled in
order to make sure they produce results. What really happens? People spend more
time trying to protect themselves than working productively, or they seek to ease
their own fear and feelings of worthlessness by hurting others.

People justify repression by the short-term results it seems to achieve.
Whip someone and he will, for a while, run faster. But the appearance of success
masks the eventual failure. The more a person is whipped, the more they harden
themselves against pain, so the whipping loses effectiveness.

This should be obvious. What is less obvious is that high ideals, when
enforced on people and not allowed to grow from them, are just another form of
repression. "You must be good" is just another way of saying "You must not be
bad."

Thus the wise ruler acts according to the best principles but doesn't preach
them; is strong, but not punishing; is purposeful, but still flexible; is clear, but
not dazzling.

What long-term results does repression produce in a work team? The same
results that manipulation and pressure produce in selling and negotiation: low
quality, poor service, and, if repression is extreme, sabotage or passive resistance.

As a sales manager, every time you yell at people or belittle them, you lower
their sales and your group's productivity. The more you yell, the more you need
to yell. Threaten people and you numb them into doing as little as possible in
order to protect themselves.

德 *A simple question: do you practice what you preach? If the*
answer is "no," you're probably the kind of manager that drove
you crazy as a sales rep. Suppose you allow yourself to do better than that?
If the answer is "yes," it's even simpler. Stop preaching entirely; just prac-
tice. Actions speak louder than words (and are more credible, anyway).

59 · MODERATION

The mark of a moderate man is freedom from his own ideas.
STEPHEN MITCHELL

To govern others well, it is first necessary to moderate one's own thinking.

Moderation means balance—avoiding the prison of one's past thoughts and experiences, and the trap of future expectations and desires—living thoughtfully and purposefully in the present.

Balance is natural. The sky does not fear the dark and praise the light. The mountain does not wish to flow like a stream.

What is unnatural? The frantic swings of thought and action, the blind allegiance to plans which have failed—but now have a punishing life of their own.

What is unnatural? The desperate submission to ideas which clearly do not work but now must be followed because they are "policy."

———

MODERATION AND BALANCE in thinking allow one to plan for the unplannable—to be able to act decisively when the unpredictable becomes reality.

德 *The first step in freeing yourself to act decisively is to sever the bonds of the past. The problem is simply in the desire to control things. Release that desire and you will become free to act, powerfully, using all your resources.*

A second step is to increase your awareness of where you are in the present by paying attention to your feelings. Are you swinging wildly like a pendulum, or calm and focused? If you feel out of balance, then stop trying so hard to do things. Stop pushing your own desires and inciting others to push back. How do you stop swinging wildly out of control? By stopping.

A third step is to bring more balance to the world around you. Gently question ideas, instead of fighting them. Offer suggestions rather than mandates. Allow others to challenge your own thinking and invite them to challenge their own. It should be obvious that no one person (or group of people) has enough brilliance to see clearly into the future or enough unclouded judgment to understand the past.

60. NOT MANAGING THINGS

Governing a large country
is like frying a small fish.
You spoil it with too much poking.

STEPHEN MITCHELL

The key to managing things in a shifting, confusing world is to stop trying to manage them. Be centered, and the confusion will gradually settle around you.

Is there danger around you? Fight it and you give it strength. Step calmly out of its way and it will dissipate by itself.

―――――

When it comes to establishing rules and regulations, everyone, high and low, should be treated alike.

SUN TZU

NOTICE IF YOU ARE TAKING responsibility away from the members of your team. What happens when decisions need to be made? Who makes them—the person closest to the customer and the situation, or somebody several levels removed? If a team member asks you, "What should I do?" remember to turn it back to the salesperson. "Good question. What should you do?"

Pay attention to the rules and procedures you establish, and the number of exceptions those rules may generate. Consider replacing all the rules with a few simple principles that center on issues of integrity and excellent service. Then, in your own daily actions, be the model of these principles. Help your people use these principles in resolving service and sales dilemmas. The "RATER" categories in Chapter 45 on page 70 are a good place to start. Turn them into an internal code of conduct so that your sales team treats each other the same way they treat customers.

Look at the reports your team members have to fill out. Whose needs are being served by the generation of this information? How much time taken away from direct contact with customers and prospects does assembling this information require? Imagine that you had the freedom to reduce reports to the essential information you needed to measure. Imagine you had the courage to run the business just on this information. Ask your boss for the freedom; ask yourself for the courage.

德 *Spend a day simply noticing how your people treat each other, without commenting or interfering. That's how they treat clients. Now imagine you could videotape your own interactions with your people. That's where they learn how to treat both each other and their customers.*

61 . HUMILITY

A great, powerful country is like the ocean, gathering all the strength of the rivers and streams into itself. Unlike most countries, the ocean does not boast of its power, it just possesses it.

Whatever power we boast of is an illusion of the moment. We should know this. The more success we achieve, the more vulnerable we are to failure.

A truly powerful person knows that power is grounded in humility.

I'M WORKING WITH A CLIENT right now who has made great strides in building an entire corporate culture based on empowerment and excellent service. A key in that development was transforming how things happened between people at the top levels of management. That meant replacing blame ("It's not my fault"), selfishness ("That's not my job; I'm too busy to help"), helplessness ("I don't have the resources to do it right"), irresponsibility ("I sent the memo; it's not my fault if you didn't understand it"), and victimization ("They are the problem, not me"), with accountability and commitment.

The owner of the company supported the changes and agreed to play by the same rules for good communication and shared commitments as everyone else, and the organization's profit, teamwork, and morale grew steadily. So did the initiative employees and managers were willing to take on their own—until the owner started feeling "left out of the loop," as if he had "lost his own company."

His response was to reassert top-down control, and to express his fear in the form of anger and intimidation; he then got frustrated by the drop in profits, morale, and teamwork. Humility would allow him to place the success of the organization first, and to gain self-satisfaction from the accomplishments of the entire team.

As a manager, be the first to recognize your mistakes and to value those people who point them out. Understanding the mistake, be quick to admit it and quick to correct it. See yourself and your own weaknesses in the people you oppose.

Humility is not the same thing as servility or absence of ego. Rather it is the recognition of the common humanity we all share with all people, and the life we share with all creation.

德 *If you constantly talk about "we," take time to check your intentions. Often when we turn WE over and examine it honestly, it says ME. If you are saying "you" a lot, in anger, check to see if "you" isn't really ME.*

Because the truth is, and is timelessly everywhere, it is the good person's treasure. The more one gives away, the more one has to give. The truth is also the "bad" person's hope, because it is always there, ready to be accepted and acted upon.

———————

How to "manage" your boss? Act simply, clearly, compassionately, and calmly. Trust that by being most fully yourself, you will accomplish more than by driving yourself crazy trying to please someone who may never be pleased or impress people who value only their own accomplishments.

When you allow yourself to trust, if you need something—help, insight, clarity of purpose—it will be there for you. When you make a mistake, you will be able to let go of guilt and defensiveness—the most serious "mistakes."

Do not be tempted to offer meaningless praise. Do not be reluctant to offer support when it is needed. Do not be tempted to say "Yes" when you know "Yes" would be harmful. Do not be reluctant to say "No" when "No" would accomplish positive results.

Saying "No" need not be confrontational. If you remember the negotiation technique "Easy on People, Tough on Positions," the same approaches will work in negotiating with your boss. "Sure, we could do that. How do we handle ... [the negative consequences?]"

Ask for what you need. "In order for me to accomplish [your or your group's goals] I need you to [state the leadership and support required from your boss for the goals to be achieved.]"

"Manage" your boss the way you "manage" your team. "Manage" your team the way you "manage" your best customer relationships. "Manage" your customers the way you "manage" yourself.

德 *How truthful are you with your boss? Can your boss count on you to act with integrity, no matter how difficult the situation? Is your integrity strong enough to stand up to the days when your boss isn't seeing things clearly, or is about to make a mistake in judgment that could hurt the entire group? Find a way to tell an important truth to your boss today, as simply and compassionately as possible.*

Simplicity, clarity, compassion, calm: these help us see the larger meaning in isolated events and reduce big problems to small, manageable essentials. In this way, difficult tasks which confound others are handled easily by a series of small, effortless actions.

For a system to remain alive, for the universe to move onward, information must be continually generated. If there is nothing new, if the information that exists merely confirms what is, then the result will be death. Isolated systems wind down and decay, victims of the laws of entropy. The fuel of life is new information—novelty—ordered into new structures.... Not management {of information} but encouragement, not control but genesis.

MARGARET WHEATLEY

WE SAY THAT SOMEONE who has trouble getting things done has "lost perspective." When that happens to us, it really means we have lost our ability to see both in depth and detail.

Your organization will "talk" to you if you listen. Signs that you need to re-examine the quality of your leadership behaviors include:

- You don't have a high degree of confidence in the ability of people below you to understand your vision, carry it out, or meet your standards for performance.
- You have to make decisions for people that, ideally, they ought to make for themselves (or you're reluctant to trust your people with important decisions).
- You are doing more "hands on" work than you'd like, and less overall leadership of the organization than you think is necessary.
- You've told people what you want repeatedly, but they don't seem to "get it."
- Your sales are going up but your costs seem to increase also; growth in the market doesn't bring commensurate profits.
- You hear a lot of excuses, blaming, and denial of accountability from customers and employees.
- It takes too long to get a straight answer to a simple question; when you do get an answer, you're not sure if you can trust it.
- Your customers tell you you're hard to work with (or you suspect you may be difficult to deal with and don't want to ask).

德 *Spend a week asking each member of your immediate team, "What's the mission of our group?" without commenting. Just listen. Their answers will tell you how you need to grow.*

Practicing:
LEADING BY FOLLOWING

1.   **Don't just do something, stand there**
As a leader you are the model for how people behave around you. Your daily actions set both the tone and standards for everyone else. If you take a stand on values and principles, others will develop the courage to do the same. If you don't take a stand, expect that no one else will either.

2.   **Simplify all actions and behaviors to a few concrete principles**
Let the values guide the results. If you want your work team to follow the principles and honor the values, let them decide what those values and principles will be. Bringing in "experts" to create the "rules" is crazy. Once the experts create the rules, they leave, taking both the rules and your money with them. Proclaiming the rules and principles "top-down" usually results only in refining the level of hypocrisy and cynicism present in the organization. Remember that a fish rots from the head down.

3.   **Take responsibility for measuring the integrity of the organization yourself**
The useful thing about "management by values" is that each time you interact with another member of the team or organization, you can check to see how that person's doing. No spread sheet or report gives you such immediate and useful feedback. Jack Welch's famous principles, "Speed, Simplicity, Self-Confidence" are good examples (for Jack Welch—your organization needs its own principles, not his). If someone said, "It's going to take months to do this," you might need to work with that person on the issue of Speed. Ask: "How can we do a high-quality job faster?" If the team member replies "I can't work any faster because of those people [in department X]," he needs support in Self-Confidence. "How can you get them to give you the cooperation you need?"

   It's even easier when your values include interpersonal principles such as "No blame." "Own the problem, don't moan about it." "Take the issue to the person who can help you resolve it." If a colleague or team member brings a problem to you to solve, don't play along. Remind the person of the principle: "Take the issue to the person who can help you resolve it."

   If someone starts blaming others, ask "What might be your part in all this? How can you turn this from a negative to a positive?" If managers persist in "beating up on people" or using threats and intimidation to get what they want, remind them of the values and principles and then offer your support in return for their commitment to change. But don't "negotiate" the values.

   You are the steward for these values and principles. Deal with problem situations immediately. If someone, after real and reasonable offers of support, chooses not to commit to the principles and values by which the organization operates, honor that choice, and ask the person to leave.

4. **Confront your own concerns and fears about authority in a caring, open way**

"Empowerment" can be threatening. The very promise of sharing power awakens all sorts of desires and expectations within a work group, some of them positive, some of them not. It's disconcerting to see an organization take on its own life, purpose, and direction, especially when it appears to move in ways you hadn't thought of or may be uncomfortable with. If you've held power, releasing it can make you feel naked.

If you hold a leadership role, you are certainly responsible to the organization for concrete results. Remember that you have chosen to accomplish these results by means of core values and principles, not in spite of them. The obligation still exists. But now you have a choice in how you satisfy it. That choice still allows you to say: "I understand the differences of opinion here. I'm asking your support for the course of action I've selected."

5. **Measure what matters**

Organizations that measure only the bottom line or, worse, sales volume, are operating by blind guesswork. Businesses operate with four sources of capital: Financial, Human, Knowledge, and Service Capital. Concentrating on just one is like trying to maintain a healthy life-style (or cure a sick person) by monitoring one of the core body systems (such as blood cholesterol level) and ignoring all the others. You can die from pneumonia, cancer, a fatal workplace accident, or a stress-induced heart attack and still have perfectly healthy blood.

- Financial Capital comprises the value of all the dollars that flow through the organization, not merely those captured by formal accounting systems. Waste, inefficient work processes, duplication of effort, etc., are usually assumed to be just another "cost of doing business." The real bottom line needs to measure all the costs and all the revenues (such as individual initiative, group creativity, shared expertise, and customer loyalty).
- Human Capital is the value of the commitments made by all employees to the organization's success. Like financial capital, it either appreciates or depreciates in value.
- Knowledge Capital is the collective wisdom and "know how" within the organization. The systems and procedures by which people communicate either share and enhance this collective knowledge or hoard and limit it.
- Service Capital is the level of quality you offer customers as perceived by your customers. Your account is either earning more capital every time your organization interacts with a customer, or losing it. Lost service capital is never regained. Annoy enough customers and you'll start a run on the bank.
- Put everybody in the organization in charge of the numbers. If they don't understand the meaning of earnings, expenses, and profits, teach them.

- Share all information that impacts the organization's effectiveness; no secrets. Since knowledge is capital, anyone who hoards, misrepresents, or misuses information is stealing from the organization. Treat this situation just as seriously as if it were money being stolen.
- The same thing applies to human capital. Reward people who add value to others, colleagues, suppliers, or customers, the way you would someone who added to the organization's profits. Deal with people who waste human capital as you would handle those who waste financial capital.
- Make it easy for customers to give you feedback, and treat that feedback as your real bottom line. It is. People who ignore or distort that feedback are also stealing from the organization.

6. "If it ain't broke, break it"

This is popular advice from consultants, who often aren't around when the breaking happens and the pieces start falling all over the place. The key: breaking and reordering need to happen organization-wide, not top-down. The security we all wish for, even at our most visionary, bold moments, comes from the collective wisdom of the group, not the individual.

> We can encourage vital organizational ambiguity with plans that are open, visions that inspire but do not describe, and by the encouragement of questions that ask "Why?" many times over. No longer the caretakers of order, we become the facilitators of disorder. We stir things up and roil the pot, looking always for those disturbances that challenge and disrupt until, finally, things become so jumbled that we reorganize work at a new level of efficacy.
>
> MARGARET WHEATLEY

7. Replace "control" with "order"

Like the principle of wu-wei ("non-acting" action), Taoist "non-controlling control" is about establishing genuine order, not merely abandoning control. It's about establishing real structure to guide how people make daily decisions and work with each other for the good of the company. This order and structure comes from a clear, meaningful purpose and reason for the organization's existence. Order needs to transcend mere business profits to articulate the organization's real value to the community of stakeholders it serves. The trick is to engage all stakeholders in what that mission is and how, at each level of the organization, it needs to be accomplished. If you impose the mission of the company top-down, don't be surprised when the organization doesn't see things your way.

Remember the strength of core values, translated into simple behaviors. If people consistently "do things right," they'll wind up "doing the right thing." Again, this is a contract everyone in the organization needs to own up to as a price for sharing in the success and purpose of the community.

Note that really effective core values contain paradoxes. For example, you might want to live by the rule, "Everybody takes initiative to make things happen when and where they need to be done." You might also want to live by the rule, "If your action might impact others, check with them before acting in ways that could hurt them." Or, for another example, "Tell the truth; be honest in giving feedback," and "Respect all people's feelings and the value of human dignity." As an organization you will need to pay constant attention to working out these contradictions in ways that strengthen the organization.

As the leader, you are more than the model. You are the organization in microcosm. You are a "hologram" of the entire organization (as is every other employee, including the lowest paid and least experienced). How you deal with both success and failure, good and bad, confidence and self-doubt, sets the standard for everyone else.

It is my humble observation
That leaders who go down in history,
Take most of their generation with them.

CARL JAPISKE

LEARNING HOW TO "KNOW" what is unknowable and "do" what can't
be done is a matter of awareness and engagement, both of which balance
and illuminate each other. It starts with relaxed, awareness of one's self,
the other person and the situation. It is expressed in complete
engagement with one's self, others, and the situation, in as much
harmony with one's spiritual values as possible at the time. No fear of
consequences, no anxiety about what others will think or do, merely
complete engagement, and then release.

"What happened as a result of my actions within me, with the other
person, and in this situation? What can I learn from what happened?"

Awareness and engagement reconcile the male/female "opposites"
of action and feeling. They balance creative energy and regard for other's
feelings. They integrate assertiveness and collaboration. Balance helps
release the desire to take charge or to deny one's own needs. Balance
"heals" the divided self of anxiety and urgency, and frees the whole mind
to operate in harmony with the spiritual presence in the universe.

> *Not the autocracy of a single stubborn melody on the one hand. Nor
> the anarchy of unchecked noise on the other. No, a delicate balance
> between the two; an enlightened freedom.*
>
> JOHANN SEBASTIAN BACH

Awareness and engagement also exist in creative tension. Without
the tension, no creativity. We care about *what is now* because we know it
can become *was.* We love *what might be* because it expresses our oneness
with creation. *Time,* as we experience it, and *timelessness.* Complete *absorption* and reflective *distance. Being* and *doing. Essence* and *form.*

109

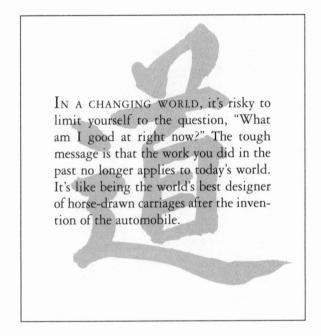

IN A CHANGING WORLD, it's risky to limit yourself to the question, "What am I good at right now?" The tough message is that the work you did in the past no longer applies to today's world. It's like being the world's best designer of horse-drawn carriages after the invention of the automobile.

Entrepreneurial Tao

64. Balance

It is easier to pull a weed than uproot a giant tree.

It is easier to gently steer a horse than to halt a wild runaway.

It is easier to balance a heavy weight with the slightest pressure of a finger than to catch it once it starts falling.

It is easier to take another step forward than worry about the entire journey.

Keep things in balance and they tend to stay in balance. Let them get out of control and the greatest effort only succeeds in sending them spinning, still out of control, in a new direction, with greater momentum.

Being balanced means being comfortable with what we have and who we are.

Creating balance means helping others gain the same sense of comfort.

———

GREG TURNER RUNS A HIGHLY SUCCESSFUL direct mail company in New Jersey. When he went into business for himself, he first figured out the values he wanted the company to stand for, then developed both a market niche and suppliers that worked with those values, and finally, used those values as the center of how employees were treated.

"We knew we couldn't compete on price against the big boys when it comes to large volume mailing because of who we are and what we stand for. Our values make our overhead too high for that. We pay our people more than our large competitors; we help our people when they're sick or need time off for personal emergencies. We really try to create more of a family atmosphere. We're a small company, we work very closely together, and we're there for 60 percent of our lives, so we have to make the workplace conducive to serving the customer first and having fun at the same time.

"So we decided that we really wanted to go after the people who do the smaller, more specialized mailings, the ones who are more concerned about quality than cheap price.

"As a result, we've gotten out of the whole mass-market mentality. We work with a lot of advertising agencies and service companies who are willing to spend more money if they know they'll get the results they need to take care of their customers. That way we've managed to eliminate a lot of competition, because even with lower prices, they can't afford to compete with us."

德 *Think about how you could translate the lessons of this story to your own business.*

65. KNOWING NOTHING

The ancient leaders knew that the more knowledge and information people amassed, the less they learned and thus the less they really knew. People who believe they have learned everything are hard to guide; people who know they know nothing guide themselves wisely and learn as they go.

———————

- Protect the right of people within your organization to disagree respectfully, but fully and completely.
- Protect people's right to say what they believe to be the truth without the fear of being punished or intimidated.
- Encourage people to voice their feelings and intuitions, especially when these appear to contradict the "facts."
- Welcome challenges to assumptions, especially your own.

One day, a poor farmer's son returned home with a fine stallion. His neighbors gathered around to congratulate him on his good fortune. "How do you know this is good fortune?" the farmer asked. Several weeks later, the horse ran away to the land of the barbarians. When the neighbors expressed their condolences, he asked "How do you know this is bad luck?" Months later, the stallion returned with a herd of fine mares, and the neighbors again were delighted with his good luck, and he asked "How do you know this isn't a catastrophe?" Sure enough, as his son was breaking in the wild horses, he fell and shattered his leg. When the neighbors expressed their sympathy, he said, "Who says this is a misfortune?" The next month, the Emperor declared war on a neighboring kingdom and conscripted all the able-bodied young men of the village. Nine-tenths of them never returned home from the war.

FROM THE *Huai Nan Tzu*

德 *Is your company a "learning organization," or is it so dependent on the lessons of the past that it can't operate wisely in the present? What are the assumptions you make about your business? Do they match your values?*

113

66. POWER

The ocean lies lower than all the rivers and draws their power into
itself.

That is the secret of the wise leader's power: to place one's self below
the people by letting go of pride. Like the leader's power, water
flows into the sea to return, endlessly, back to the rivers in rain.
Without the people's gifts, the leader has no power.

———

*If a leader is closed-minded, suspicious, and insensitive to people's true natures, he will
find a lot of things offensive. Then his bad mood goes out and fights with everybody
else's bad moods. Isn't this stupid?*

SHŌSHAN

OUR USUAL CONCEPT OF THE LEADER is the person at the top of the organizational charts, or the entrepreneurial hero out in front of everyone else, including
his or her own employees.

Perhaps it makes more sense to invert the organizational pyramid and
imagine ourselves as leaders at the bottom.

In this way the leader's power flows upward by example, not downward by
words alone. The greatest power exists at the top, at the closest point of contact
between the organization and its customers, whether they be external consumers
or internal end users.

Imagine this pyramid as a heavy weight. The leader's role now is to balance
it, to help others have more thoughtful, caring power, so that no one part of the
organization thinks more of itself than another, and values the interaction with
the customer as they would respect the relationship with a close friend.

Such a leader is truly centered. Because so much of the work happens above
the leader, he or she is freer to pay attention to the whole. (If the pyramid were a
gyroscope, its balance would be in tune with the earth's calm rotation through
time.)

Reward the people who give you the things you need to function as a
leader—clarity, commitment, truthfulness, dependability, courage, responsiveness—with their own gifts.

德 *Spend an entire week paying attention to the kinds of behavior
you notice in your employees, the kinds of behavior you typically
ignore, and the kinds of behavior you reward personally. If you keep a
journal or note pad handy, you'll be able to write down all the instances
as they happen. Imagine that the only behavior you get from people will be
what you notice and reward.*

"But these ideas are impractical. They don't make sense." Find people who are at peace with themselves and others. They will tell you the peace and purpose this awareness brings to their lives.

At the center of peacefulness lies compassion, simplicity, and patience.

Compassion allows us to feel our kinship with all people and to give them the gift of understanding we give as well to ourselves. It is only when we are compassionate that we can act courageously with others.

Simplicity allows us to act completely, fully, and powerfully according to the needs of each moment. Simplicity is the quiet point of balance in a world that spins blurringly around us or seems to rush madly ahead of us. Simplicity allows us to know when to move forward and when to retreat or when to stop acting and allow events to unfold.

Patience is the realization that we are part of a much larger, constantly unfolding process that, for all of the hurt which people bring to each other in the world, has goodness at its heart. We can allow ourselves to cooperate with that goodness instead of fighting it or pretending it doesn't exist.

––––––––––

IF YOU THINK THESE IDEAS ARE unrealistic, ask yourself what is "real." If we pick up the daily paper, we find yet another proud, powerful corporation stumbling into chaos, or oblivion, its leaders lost, torn apart by internal struggles, or swallowed in greed and self-interest. We see companies invest millions of dollars on complex strategies (often imposed on the organization by outside "experts") only to find that the strategies never work, or worse, that they accelerate the organization's failure. We see "experts" argue over the meaning of events they no longer understand or even fully grasp.

德 *Identify colleagues or employees in positions of authority with whom you are frustrated. Ask yourself: "What am I doing that contributes to the problem?" Change your part of it, notice what new opportunities open up in the relationship, and act on them in simple, compassionate ways. Be patient with others' efforts to change. They will probably take two steps forward and one step back for awhile. Reward their successes for awhile. You've probably said more than you need to about their failures already.*

Identify your anxieties about the business itself. Identify suppliers and vendors you could establish better partnerships with, and act with compassion, simplicity, and patience to strengthen those key relationships.

68. COMPETITION

To be in the world, to act as a leader, one encounters competition and opposition. How can one balance the spirit of compassion, simplicity, and patience with the need to compete?

The most dangerous opponent is the one who says the least, but acts each moment with sudden, complete power, holding nothing back, wasting no effort, only then to return to a state of poised, unassailable balance, ready to strike again.

Practice compassion and you free yourself from blinding anger. Practice simplicity and you free yourself from crippling pride. Practice patience and you free yourself from anxious haste.

Enter the mind of your opponent fully and you will know what to do. Embrace the spirit of your opponent deeply and you will find yourself.

"I ALWAYS WANT MY COMPETITORS to be at their best," a sales executive once remarked to me. "Only that way will I know I'm meeting their challenge the way I need to. That's the only time success means anything."

It's the same with competitive athletes. There is no joy in the victory over a helpless, injured, or incompetent opponent.

We have been taught that competition means beating (or even beating up on) one's opponents, and striving to be Number One. For many people, being Number One means that everyone else has to be Number Two. All too easily, the world fills up with people we need to turn into Number Two's: our competitors, our customers, our suppliers, the members of our team, our colleagues, our spouses and loved ones, our children.

- Do what you need to do and no more.
- Do it in keeping with the flow of things.
- Do it just as soon as it needs doing.
- Do it wholly and completely.
- When you're finished, stop.

德 *Write down how you feel about your competition right now, using the first words that come to your mind. If your list is predominantly negative, check how you respond to what you perceive as negative competitive pressure. Are you living your core values with your competition, or subverting and contradicting those values?*

69. YIELDING IN ORDER TO WIN

69. YIELDING IN ORDER TO WIN

The skilled martial artist knows that victory lies in yielding, and using the opponent's strength to defeat him.

In this way the martial artist attacks without advancing and counters blows without effort. The attack and the response are one fluid action. For the martial artist, no elaborate weapons are necessary because everything one needs to defend one's self is readily at hand when needed. When competition is unavoidable, the skilled strategist draws the opponent into battle.

Therefore, the greatest error is to underestimate one's opponent, since in so doing we underestimate ourselves. When we underestimate our opponent we lose our greatest strengths: compassion, simplicity, and patience.

———

THINK ABOUT THE CONFLICT SITUATIONS you're involved in, whether they exist at a strategic level against your competition, with another group within your company, within your own work team, with a spouse or a friend, or even within yourself.

If you feel driven by anger, consider whether what angers you in someone else may really be your resistance to those same qualities in yourself. The more we sustain our anger at the other person, the more we sustain the same weakness in ourselves.

If you feel shame or discouragement at a defeat, consider how quickly things change. Defeats are valuable gifts because they allow us to learn how to handle the next challenge more effectively.

If you feel pride over a victory, look at your defeated opponent and see yourself.

德 *Check your own level of accountability as a business leader by paying attention to how you explain things that go well and things that go wrong. Identify the greatest success your company has enjoyed in the past month. The greatest setback. Whom do you consider responsible? Others? Circumstances beyond your control? Focus on what you can learn from both successes and setbacks so you can start using "I" in positive ways.*

117

It's easier to write, talk, and think about these teachings than to deeply understand and confidently act on them.

As soon as we turn them into principles for living they start contradicting themselves. We turn them into a guide for living and we are instantly lost.

How to solve this riddle? Look inside yourself.

————

"Do you now understand," the Master asked me one day after a particularly good shot, "what I mean by 'it shoots,' and 'it hits'?"

"I'm afraid I don't understand anything more at all," I answered, "even the simplest things have got in a muddle. Is it 'I' who draws the bow, or is it the bow that draws me into the state of highest tension? Do 'I' hit the goal, or does the goal hit me? Is 'IT' spiritual when seen by the eyes of the body, and corporeal when seen by the eyes of the spirit—or both or neither? Bow, arrow, goal, and ego all melt into one another, so that I can no longer separate them. And even the need to separate has gone. For as soon as I take the bow and shoot, everything becomes so clear and straightforward and so ridiculously simple...."

"Now at last," the Master broke in, "the bowstring has cut right through you."

EUGEN HERRIGEL

PART OF THE DIFFICULTY IN ACCEPTING and acting on these principles results from the conflict between them and our rational minds. It helps to remember that what we call "reason" is merely that small part of existence which we see imperfectly with our limited vision and then turn into an absolute truth. If there are truthful principles anywhere in the world, they are everywhere in the world. If we can find meaning in anything, we can find it in everything. Therefore we can find it, daily, in ourselves.

德 *Identify the greatest unresolved challenge facing your company—the one that wakes you up at 4:00 a.m. from a troubled sleep. If you have created a set of core beliefs, ask how that problem could be resolved by acting courageously on what you believe. If you don't have a set of core beliefs, create one. The next time you can't sleep might not be a bad opportunity.*

Practicing:

ENTREPRENEURIAL TAO

1.   Do what you love; love what you do

With each new downsizing or technological breakthrough, thousands more "old" jobs that existed within the dying bureaucratic, paternalistic, military-style major corporations also disappear, and thousands more new "entrepreneurs" enter the market place. Trying to build a business by offering more of the same is a recipe for failure. Trying to outwit the market by coming up with the newest "pet rock" is risky. For every successful "pet" there are thousands of plain, unattractive "rocks" that no one wants.

All the ideas within the section on service (pages 67–79) help when it comes to differentiating yourself within the market. But the key is the willingness to look for the passion and energy within you as the source of your business. What do you care about? What are you willing to work at with love and commitment? The more love and commitment, the more positive energy.

2.   Make a difference for the planet

There are already more people out there trying to make money than the economy can sustain. In order to generate this money, more and more natural resources are being consumed and more and more of the complex biosphere in which we live is being polluted or destroyed. As Paul Hawken notes:

> Every day, American farmers and ranchers consume 20 billion gallons of water more than the rainfall can replace. At current levels of use, the Oglala Aquifer, an underground river underneath the Great Plains larger than any other body of fresh water on earth, will have dried up in 40 years or less. All the farm "factories" which rely on that water source will be out of water and luck at the same time (as will the people fed by the produce of those "factories"). Every year we lose 25 billion tons of topsoil, equal to all the wheat fields in Australia. And the global population keeps increasing exponentially.
>
> Every year, another 27,000 natural species on the planet are lost, (seventy-four per day, one every twenty minutes) largely as the result of the deforestation of tropical rain forests (500,000 trees are cut every hour). The "cash crops" which replace the rain forest don't grow well, and the displaced people from these natural environments choke large cities, straining economic and community resources to the breaking point. In order to wring greater yields of food supplies from the earth, we turn to chemical fertilizers which gradually strip the soil of natural nutrients, and use chemical pesticides to kill off every living thing but the food to be harvested. Increasingly often what's killed includes people. About every two minutes, one hundred people (typically in the poorer southern nations) will have died from pesticide poisoning, 25 million each year. In some Third World countries, more people die from pesticides than from disease.

119

And it's not just a "Third World" problem. The more than 500 billion tons of toxic chemicals released into the environment each year don't break down naturally. Unlike naturally created substances, they don't become "food" for some other living thing, as a dead tree feeds the soil; they kill all life. Recent studies in human fertility rates in industrialized nations indicate the real cost. The effect of toxic chemicals on the human system is grim: cancer, infertility, birth defects and still births. Within our bodies they disrupt the endocrine system and throw the immune system out of balance.

So the challenge is not merely to make more money, to take care of ourselves at the cost of everything else. The real goal is, in some way, large or small, to make a difference—to heal, or more clearly, to open ourselves to the healing gift within us all and share that gift.

All actions and all businesses can be conducted with awareness and purposefulness; it doesn't matter what the "work" itself is, so long as the real net result nourishes life and generates love.

4.   Live simply; work simply

Owe as little as possible; own as little as possible; clean up your own mess; leave no monuments behind. "Entrepreneurial Tao" reverses the assumptions and beliefs of the past century. Instead of running a business whose purpose is to accumulate wealth and fame, share the wealth and fame as widely as possible. They will come back to you tenfold, with much less effort on your part than you would have expended in seeking fame and coveting wealth.

5.   Communicate your uniqueness consistently

Everything you do, every conversation, all the physical objects from products to marketing materials to invoices, all of these tell people who you are. Either they contribute to a consistent awareness of what makes you special, or they send a blurred message that easily gets lost in the clutter of today's information-choked world.

Start again with your mission and purpose. Translate it first into daily behaviors—how you interact with everyone: prospects, clients, suppliers, the local newspaper, other local business people, the butcher, the baker, the candlestick maker. You simply do not know who will hear of you, be moved by your vision, and pass the word along.

It follows, therefore, that the more you use your vision to help others without being asked or wanting something in return, the faster that message gets out. Jay Conrad Levinson's book, *Guerrilla Marketing Excellence*, builds on these principles in specific, direct, "how-to" fashion. I like his "Guerrilla Marketing Golden Rule #43: Companies that think of what they can give to people fare better than those that think of what they can take." His application principle for this rule is even better: "Give till it helps."

### 6.	Leverage value-added networks

The case studies from people who are succeeding with their own small business-es illustrate this point. If you share with people whose resources complement yours, and provide ways to add value to your clients, you gain their capacity without the overhead. That means you can provide better service than your competition at a lower price. Greg Turner (page 110) shares a building with a company that uses laser printers. Typically they are unused at night, merely contributing to their company's overhead. He can handle unexpected rush jobs or sudden high-volume orders by using that added printing capacity when the machines are normally idle, earning income for nobody. The key is the "win/win" arrangement he created with the other owner. Here's what Levinson says about that. "Guerrilla Marketing's Golden Rule #44: To network properly, ask ques-tions, listen to answers, and focus on the problems of the people with whom you network." Not "How can you help me," but "How can I help you?" Or note that Geoff Price (page 83) began his own business as a town-wide event to help all the local merchants.

### 7.	Renew yourself continually

Remember that your organization is a living thing, not a machine. You may run it; you also serve it. It (and you) need time to breathe and laugh, opportunities to share insights and feelings, and moments for reflection and celebration.

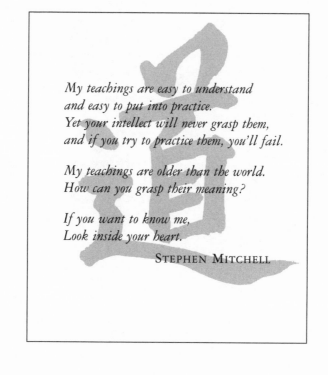

My teachings are easy to understand
and easy to put into practice.
Yet your intellect will never grasp them,
and if you try to practice them, you'll fail.

My teachings are older than the world.
How can you grasp their meaning?

If you want to know me,
Look inside your heart.

STEPHEN MITCHELL

Mastery

71. KNOWING NOTHING

Knowledge is a sophisticated statement of ignorance ...
confusion is a doorway to a new understanding.

KARL POPPER

Really smart people know how little they know. It follows then, that the greatest wisdom is "knowing" nothing at all.

Thinking you understand more than you do is unhealthy—for you and others. You make yourself and others sick. If you understand sickness, then you can begin to become healthy.

———

WHEN OTHER PEOPLE ASK, "What should I do?" any answer we give sustains them in a state of dependency and powerlessness. The smart, healthy answer is, "I don't know. What do you want to do?" The helpful follow-up questions are the simple ones that assist clients in achieving their own clarity.

- What does that mean to you?
- Why is getting it important to you?
- How will you feel if you do it?

The same process works for "How should I do it?" in all its related forms: "What's the best way...?" "What's the safest way...?" "What's the easiest way...?" "What's the right way...?"

Clients often bring us their own doubts as questions for us to solve for them. "Give me proof that this will absolutely work 100 percent with no risk to me whatsoever." Any time we have tried to reassure these kinds of doubts, we know how useless this effort is. Every proof generates two more doubts. "Well, I know it worked there, but can you prove it will work here?" "It may have worked then. Are you convinced it will work now?" These doubts are the client's issues to solve. The only honest answer is "It may, and it may not. I don't know for sure. But I think it's the best option. What do you think is the best course to take?"

 Take a firm stand on a difficult, uncertain issue based solely on your principles, not on what you "know."

72. TEACHING NOTHING

Therefore the Master steps back
so that people won't be confused.
{The Master} teaches without a teaching,
so that people will have nothing to learn.

STEPHEN MITCHELL

THE MORE WE TRUST OURSELVES, the more others are able to trust us. This trust starts with our refusal to make decisions for other people. It gets more difficult when we believe there's important knowledge or information a client or customer needs in order to make a sound decision about his or her future. Knowledge is always a tool, never a solution. A carpenter never confuses the hammer and the house, or a hammer with a saw.

> *When I asked the Master how we could get on without him on our return to Europe, he said: "Your question is already answered by the fact that I made you take a test. You have now reached the stage where teacher and pupil are no longer two persons, but one. You can separate from me any time you wish. Even if broad seas lie between us, I shall always be with you when you practice what you have learned. I need not ask you to keep up with your regular practicing, not to discontinue it on any pretext whatsoever, and to let no day go by without your performing the ceremony, even without bow and arrow, or at least without having breathed properly. I need not ask you because I know you can never give up this spiritual archery.*

EUGEN HERRIGEL

———————

ONE WAY TO "GIVE" THE information is to see if it already exists, in some useful form, in customers' minds. Another gift is to clarify the choices a client faces, as clearly and compassionately as possible.

But the real gift is helping clients "forget" or "unlearn" what they've just been "taught" by allowing them to take ownership of the consequences of their choices and actions.

德 *Identify a client relationship based on dependency—in which both you and the client gain satisfaction from relying on your expertise and experience as a "teacher." Help the client assume greater responsibility for his or her future.*

73. PREACHING NOTHING

We know that misfortune exists in the world. Floods and storms ravage both homes and farmlands; the weapons that angry men fire at each other kill innocent children; great cities sink into decay; strong companies collapse into dust; and every life ends in death. This pain can cause us to do more harm than good in trying to "right" what we believe are "wrongs."

We call these things misfortunes because they run against our hopes for the incredibly short time we are alive in this world. We start preaching what others should do and how they should act.

Nature is wiser. It watches the leaf nourish the tree for a time as it turns sunlight and rain into life-supporting sap, then fall to the ground and nourish the earth. In the same way, over time, the fallen tree nourishes the sapling.

Try as we may, we simply cannot control the future or change the past. All we have is each moment in which to live as thoughtfully and caringly as we can. In itself, is this not enough of a gift?

———

THE POWER OF SELFLESSNESS was made clear to me some years ago by a friend, Joe Masterson, of the Teare Group, a benefits and human-resource consulting firm in New Jersey. In 1987, as a highly successful small group medical sales manager for a major insurance company, he tuned into a headquarters conference call with the rest of the sales force and learned that the company had decided to get out of his field completely. He and all the rest of the sales force were out of a job. After the initial shock wore off, like all the other reps, he started looking for a new job. What made his search easy was the three years of networking he had engaged in as he watched his company's position in the market become more difficult. Unlike most networking, Joe's was "value-added." Wherever he could, with no immediate thought of return or "give back," he had helped clients, suppliers, even some competitors, figure out how to do things better, faster, smarter, or more profitably. These gifts came back when he lost his job. The consulting revenues he earned doing his job search, all initiated by networking friends, allowed him to bank his severance pay, and within six months he had a better-paying job that allowed him to eventually form his own, successful company. Simple. Effortless.

德 Confront a tough spiritual challenge or a major personal doubt you have about yourself. What gifts have you been given that will allow you to meet this challenge or self-doubt with greater courage and clarity of purpose?

126

74. CONTROLLING NOTHING

A master carpenter created our world. When we try to control things we pick up the master's tools as if they were our own. What arrogance. Play with the master's tools and you'll only cut your hands.

———————

SINCE THE ENTIRE UNIVERSE is interconnected, every action you take produces change of some kind or other. Even the action of merely observing something changes both you and what you observe. Control, therefore, is a myth.

Either we are interconnected, timelessly, with all creation, or we are terrifyingly finite and alone. Your choice is to replace control with awareness and faith.

Center your actions around strong values grounded in the well-being of all living things. Serve these values.

Deepen your understanding of what's really happening by encouraging and rewarding truthful feedback from all the people you work with. Make it "safe" and "easy" for all assumptions to be challenged, especially your own. Let your body "talk" to you and listen to what it says. Internal anxiety and stress, anger and helplessness are sure signs that you are trying to control something that can't be controlled. Let your organization "talk" to you and listen to what it says. Anxiety, stress, anger, and blame carry the same meaning within the living entity of organizations.

Once you accept constant change, letting go of the desire to control becomes easier.

德 *Look at situations you are currently trying to control or "make happen." Ask yourself what you would do if, instead, you acted with calm faith. Take these actions.*

Empowerment embodies the belief that the answer to the latest crisis lies within each of us and therefore we all buckle up for adventure. Empowerment bets that people at our own level or below will know best how to organize to save a dollar, serve a customer, and get it right the first time.... This requires a belief that my safety and freedom are in my own hands. No easy task, therefore the adventure.

PETER BLOCK

When taxes increase, people starve.

When governments start "governing," people rebel, and lose their independence.

The more leaders do for people, the less people do for themselves.

Control breeds resistance and fosters dependency. The best way to help people is to trust them and leave them alone.

IF YOUR ORGANIZATION and your immediate network are grounded in solid principles, have faith in those principles. Allow them to flourish by removing the unnecessary "controls" and making it easier for other people to make good choices. Let the principles do the work.

Lauren Anderson headed up Estée Lauder's sales training for years, and was one of the architects of their highly successful summer "university" at Vassar College. Now she leads her own consulting company. But she started out, like so many others, "behind the counter." She tells this story of "principle-based" selling. As a young woman, she started working in a "high-class" department store in Texas. She noticed a plainly-dressed Mexican woman walk into the store, look around, wait for service, and then, having been ignored, leave. Her manager commented, "I hate those people coming in here. She's probably going to shoplift something. Ignore her and maybe she'll go away." On the third day the woman stopped in. Lauren went up to her, as she would to any customer, and sincerely and politely offered to help. The woman, a wealthy and well-respected member of the Hispanic community, not only made several major purchases, she brought her friends, and Lauren's business soared. "I never let myself forget that lesson," Lauren remarks. "You simply have to look past assumptions and prejudices and see the person that's really there."

德 *Let the people you care about the most make their own choices in life. Let them experience for themselves the consequences of these choices. Extend this same love and freedom to all people.*

Consider how we enter the world—supple, warm, and pliable. Consider how we leave it—stiff, cold, and hard. Plants grow green, tender, and flexible; they die withered and brittle.

If we choose to be stiff and inflexible we choose to ally ourselves with death and experience that death every day. If we choose to be supple, warm, and pliable, we choose to ally ourselves with life— not just the life we experience but the life we came from and will return to.

———

A STUDENT CAME BEFORE THE MASTER Bankei and asked to be helped in getting rid of his violent temper.

"Show me this temper," said Bankei. "It sounds very fascinating."

"I haven't got it right now, so I can't show it to you," said the student.

"Well then," said Bankei, "bring it to me when you have it."

"But I can't bring it just when I happen to have it," protested the student. "I'd surely lose it again before I got it to you."

"In such a case," said Bankei, "it seems to me that this temper is not part of you, it must come into you from outside. I suggest that whenever it gets into you, you beat yourself with a stick until the temper can't stand it, and runs away."

德 *Begin each day with thankfulness. You are alive, and have an entire day ahead of you to live as completely, compassionately, and thoughtfully as possible. It is only our fear and lack of trust that causes us to feel we are worse off than others or better than them.*

Nurture awareness and thankfulness during the day. Often that requires nothing more than paying attention to what is happening around us that, on its own terms, is worthwhile and beautiful. "Schedule" time in the day for reflection, meditation, purposeful feedback, and exchange with others that has insight as its goal. Once each hour, relax and breathe deeply for five minutes. It is only our fear and lack of trust that causes us to focus on what we feel is "bad," or "ugly," or "harmful."

End the day with awareness and thankfulness. Writing a daily journal helps. So does reading from a book of meditations or other spiritual thoughts. It is only our fear and lack of trust that makes us believe our actions are useless and our lives inconsequential.

77. NO CREDIT

What kind of person is it
Who has more than he needs
And so gives it out, and gives it freely?

Only a being that is filled with the Tao.
MAN-HO KWOK, MARTIN PALMER, JACK RAMSAY

IF EVERYTHING WE HAVE IS A GIFT, why take credit for sharing it?

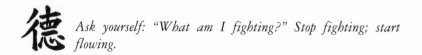 *Ask yourself: "What are the gifts I have been given to share with others?" Ask the same question of people you trust. Assume that the gift you enjoy is inexhaustible—a well that will not run dry. Find a brand new person to share that gift with in some significant way each day.*

78. NO STRUGGLE

Nothing is softer and more yielding than water, yet over time water turns mountains to sand. In time, soft overcomes hard, weak overcomes strong, flexible overcomes rigid. We know this is true but struggle to put it into practice. Perhaps we should stop struggling.

In the midst of sorrow, be serene. In the midst of anger, be calm. In the midst of evil, be good. In the midst of despair, be steady. In the midst of confusion, be clear. The truth is a paradox.

Ask yourself: "What am I fighting?" Stop fighting; start flowing.

79. NO BLAME

Failure is an opportunity.
If you blame someone else,
there is no end to the blame.

STEPHEN MITCHELL

IF WE LET GO THE DESIRE to be better than other people, we release ourselves from the pressure of being worse. We were no better than anyone else when we entered the world and will be no better when we leave it.

德 *How would you act if you knew no one would ever see your actions? If you knew there would be no consequences, good or bad? No prize, no penalty? Act this way in the presence of both "good" and "bad," and when "prizes" and "penalties" are greatest.*

80. NO ANXIETY

If you want to be free, learn to live simply.

JOHN HEIDER

WE KILL OURSELVES AT WORK so that we can retire to live in peace. That seems backward. "Retirement" can be more than something we desire for the future; understood fully it can be something to enjoy each day. If we "retire" inward to peacefulness, the world becomes peaceful around us. When we love the work we do, it ceases to be "work."

德 *Empty yourself fully and completely into each moment as if there were no time, no future, no past. Just now. Enjoy its richness. When it's over, let go completely.*

81. No Urgency

The wisdom that we seek is simple, not showy or eloquent. Showy eloquence is foolish, not wise. People who understand this do not seek to persuade others. People who need to persuade, understand nothing. People who share this awareness with others enjoy abundance. People who seek to grasp it for themselves wind up empty-handed.

We are beginning our own voyage to discover the new world. All we need is our own willingness to begin the adventure and live with the consequences. Besides, sleeping peacefully through the night is overrated.

PETER BLOCK

德 *Benefit others without causing harm; nourish without demanding; act on others' behalf, not in opposition to them; tread gently on the earth, leave no tracks.*

Practicing:

MASTERY

It is easier to act yourself into a new way of thinking than think yourself into a new way of acting.

DEVELOPING ONE'S FULL POTENTIAL as a salesperson—or simply as a person—is a life-long discipline, and, at the same time, a matter of simple daily practice. It takes more sustained commitment that any "magic diet" such as those offered by popular books and tapes on selling. It's rather like the decision to eat simple, balanced meals each day.

An old Zen teaching says, "Mastery is simple. Eat when you're hungry, sleep when you're tired, and move your bowels when they're full. Superficial people will laugh at this, but the truth is simple."

The eleven lessons which follow can serve as a life-long guide to personal growth. Your "teacher" is yourself. When you feel anxious, angry, or defeated as a salesperson, find a lesson on this page that you have allowed yourself to forget, and renew your commitment to practicing selling in an easier, more caring, trustful way. Each time you are with a client, or any other person, treat each of these as a gift to share. Learn from the gift each time you give it.

1. **Knowing Nothing:** I don't have the right answer for you; find your own way.

2. **Teaching Nothing:** I can't teach you anything; discover it for yourself.

3. **Preaching Nothing:** Find your own "right" and "wrong."

4. **Controlling Nothing:** I don't control the future; choose for yourself.

5. **Controlling No One:** I'm not controlling you; you are free.

6. **No Resistance:** No "should"s; there's nothing to rebel against.

7. **No Credit:** I want no credit for what I do; there are no strings attached.

8. **No Struggle:** I'm not here to help you; you're here to help you.

9. **No Blame:** I don't blame you; I don't blame myself.

10. **No Anxiety:** I am content with what I have; no cause for fear.

11. **No Urgency:** I have nothing to say, nothing to covet, nothing to argue about, and nothing to do.

ROZ PARRY IS A CONSULTANT IN communication and team building. She's also owner and president of Roz Parry Public Relations, RPPR, in Reno, Nevada. In talking with Candy Pearce, a candidate for Reno City Council over lunch one day, the conversation turned to the need for people in public office to have not just brains but heart, and to understand not only how things work but why. Candy had run for city council in 1993 in a vicious race highlighted by "attack commercials" and tough negative campaigning, and lost. The effect of the personal attacks was devastating to her. It's one thing to say, "But I'm not that person." It's another to know that thousands of people have only that biased viewpoint as the source of their belief. In 1995 Candy decided to run again, but this time on a positive campaign. The pain of having to face negative attacks was still very real for her.

"I know if I go in again, I'll get attacked, just as before. I'm a threat to all the people who have controlled things and had everything their way. I don't want to sink to that level, but I don't know what else to do. I know I have to stay positive. That's the only way I 'win' from the perspective of my own spiritual development. But how do you counter a negative campaign in positive ways—and still win the election?"

Roz's feedback was simple. "Pay attention to your conscience—what you know is right. Stay focused on why you got into this in the first place, not what people are doing to you. If your message really is what the voters want, then if your being true to your message, you're also being true to what's best in this community."

Candy decided to base her campaign on reaching people personally—maximizing personal contact by working door-to-door as opposed to the competition's "attack ads" in TV, newspaper, and direct mail. In her TV spots, she refused to "pick up the gauntlet." Instead, she focused on the character issue, relying on testimonials from local people who spoke simply and eloquently about her intelligence, capability, and deep concern for the community. The nastier the opposition became, the calmer and more focused she stayed. In the election, Candy won by the largest margin of any candidate, in both the primary and final elections, against opponents who were endorsed by the local big business establishment and had controlled politics in the town for decades.

Roz sees Candy's election as an example of *The Tao of Sales* in action. "You have to be true to your deep beliefs, especially in the face of adversity. That way, you attract the people to you who value you and what you stand for. They come to you, not the other way around. It starts with faith in yourself, faith in your beliefs, and faith that the universe will respond. It's not easy, especially when clients aren't there. In the down times one can be frightened that the up times won't return. That's when faith steps in. I have to remind myself that wu wei works. We all believe we have to be a hamster in a wheel. I have to stop and remind myself that the clients who are going to come to me will find me."

Simple Selling

THIS CHAPTER IS ABOUT doing things *with* customers, not *to* them. Instead of control, it works toward partnership. It uses a core model to describe the overall flow of a successful sales call, but in the same way a skier might look at a challenging slope before skiing it or a white water rafter might look at rapids before starting the run. Planning one's route is important, but working with the slope and the feel of the snow, or with the constantly changing surge and flow of the river, is what makes the run possible, and enjoyable.

The model begins in the customers' world, with the decisions a customer will need to make in order to reach the decision to buy with confidence and commitment. Years ago, Larry Wilson gave us a picture of that decision chain in terms of the obstacles a salesperson needs to work through:

NO TRUST | "I'm not sure about your motives and intentions, so I'm not going to open up very much."

NO PROBLEM | "I think everything's basically okay the way it is. I don't have any needs. I may have problems, but I don't have the means of solving them and I doubt you can help me very much. I have problems, but the way I'm handling them is okay right now."

NO SOLUTION | "I know there's a problem, but you can't solve it. I know there's a problem, but your solution is too risky, too expensive, too impractical. And it's your solution. I want to find my solution."

NO COMMITMENT | "I know there's a problem, I understand your solution, but the potential benefits don't outweigh the possible risks."

To these obstacles, we have added a fifth—lack of energy and commitment to working in partnership with the salesperson toward a solution.

NO COLLABORATION | Customers who say "You solve my problem for me," deny their accountability for the eventual solution and invite us to assume a responsibility we can never meet. This obstacle is most punishing in service selling because the customer is ultimately responsible for how well the service functions after it's been bought. Often customers ask us to be the "experts" and tell them what they should do. In difficult times, it eases their burden of choice and responsibility for outcomes. That makes it a shaky and unreliable basis for delivering excellent, long-term service.

The sales model that evolved was the result of fifteen years' work with over 8,000 salespeople, in many industries, from technological products and services to retail sales and investment services.

In January, in conversation with a friend who had attended a seminar developed by the Traditional Acupuncture Institute (TAI) of Columbia, MD, we learned of a much older model whose symmetry with what we were teaching and sharing with clients was startling.

This model, thousands of years old, is the "whole system" portrayal of the five elements and seasons which underpins traditional Chinese acupuncture and spiritual healing. Besides representing the cycle of yearly seasons, from autumn through winter to late summer, it harmonizes as well the "inner seasons" of discovery, personal growth, collaborative learning, and partnership. This same integrity or harmony applies to the five elements, which, when in balance, stimulate health in mind, spirit, and body—the essence of Taoist existence.

METAL—Autumn
Honoring All Concerned (Acknowledgment)
Insight into who I am and who the other is in these circumstances.

WATER—Winter
Knowledge (Wisdom)
Willingness to be in inquiry, to be in unknowing.

WOOD— Spring
Intention (Vision)
Seeing what the other's vision is—clarity about the intention.

FIRE— Summer
Partnership (Warmth)
Opening the heart to create partnership.

EARTH—Late Summer
Agreement (Consideration).
Mutual agreement about what I can offer you that would serve you.

The "healthiness" of this model underscores what years of working with salespeople has taught us: that a shared, collaborative, creative partnership between buyer and seller follows its own internal logic or "flow," working *with* the natural buying process in the customer or client's mind, not *against* it.

In nature, of course, the seasons are a cycle. Within humans, all elements are balanced (or out of balance). In a sales cycle, there is a starting place, and a culmination that represents the growth of empathy, knowledge, vision, partnership, and commitment. In a strong, on-going sales relationship, this cycle renews itself over time, just as all living things do.

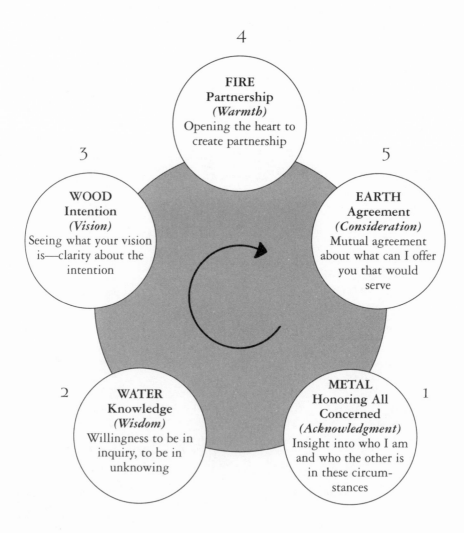

The sales model with the acronym "CLASS" appears below. Like the cycle of seasons, it begins with Connection: acknowledgment, and ends with Support: agreement.

CONNECT: Begin the sales meeting in a state of relaxed, attentive acknowledgment. Be willing to understand, care about, and value customers' initial concerns and points of view—especially when the customer seems initially to disagree or resist you. Take the initiative of modeling the kind of relationship you want to establish with the customer.

LEARN: Help the customer identify real needs and priority goals. Since this may require challenging the customers' current understanding of things, you'll need the rapport you've begun to develop. Remember that it's not enough merely to learn what customers believe they want. You need to help them discover what's most important to them. Work with your customers to clarify more deeply the gap between what they have now and what they really desire. Help them begin to understand the cost to them of not acting on their best interests. Clarify with them the value of what they could have or achieve. Stay open to discovery.

AGREE: Define, as specifically as possible, the positive goal your customers would like to achieve and your joint responsibility in meeting that goal. Before trying to provide a way for customers to reach their goals, confirm that you both understand the goal and are committed to working together toward achieving it. Treat this step as a "breathing place" in the sales process for both people to get clear about the value of making something positive happen together. Clarify your shared intentions.

SHARE: Work with the customer to find a way to reach this goal using your products and services. Allow the customer to become part of the discovery and decision-making process. Reinforce the value of making the effort to achieve the goal. If your products or services aren't the best way for the customer to meet his or her goal, say so.

SUPPORT: Trade your support and service for the customers' commitment to act. Truthfully acknowledge the risks involved with the customers' decision to buy. Be clear about what customers need to do to get value out of what they've purchased. We don't live in a world of product guarantees any more. The only thing you can guarantee is your support after the sale has been made. Use that support to help customers make the decision to commit.

CONNECT:

- Ask opening questions that invite the customer to talk at length about feelings, needs, and perceived problems.

- Demonstrate your willingness to understand and value the customer through compassionate, patient listening. This listening includes taking the time to reflect back to the customer, in the customer's own language, your understanding of those feelings, needs, and perceived problems.

- Self–disclosure: Make the simplest, clearest statement you can about your deep values and your commitment to work in partnership with your customers toward achieving their goals.

- Adding value: Use your research and industry knowledge to provide insight and information to the customer as a gift—with no strings attached. You are modeling the kind of service you will provide throughout the entire sales relationship.

LEARN:

- Take time for patient, persistent exploration of the meaning of what you're hearing from the customer. The purpose is not merely to understand the customer's problem well enough to propose a solution. It's for both of you to clarify the customer's real goals, the value of achieving them, and the cost of failing to do so.

- Model the courage you want from the customer: You're "selling" shared responsibility for the customer's success. Some customers may not want to buy that. They may want you to take all the responsibility for the sale (so you get all the blame if things go wrong). You need to say "no" to that offer.

- Model the integrity you want from the customer: Remind the customer that if you discover that what you're selling won't meet the customer's needs and goals, you'll either modify it so it will or tell the customer you can't help.

- Be willing to "be in unknowing," to explore without needing to have an answer, to identify conflicts without having to resolve them, to sense opportunities for an immediate sale without needing to act immediately upon them.

AGREE:

- Test the level of courage and commitment both of you need to achieve in order to work toward the customer's goals. Be clear about what you're both getting in return for that courage and commitment. Be clear about your intentions.

- Ask for the customer's agreement to proceed, as collaborative partners, toward finding a way to meet the customer's needs. Ask about the customer's intentions.

- If the customer doesn't want to make that commitment, think hard about whether you want to go the distance alone.

SHARE:

- Help your customers figure out how your products and service can become a vehicle for reaching their goals. You're trying to create a "solution" with the customer, using what you know or might provide as part of the "answer."

- Allow the "solution" to evolve truthfully and creatively.

- Keep sharing the responsibility with the customer by focusing on what you both need to do to make a successful outcome possible.

SUPPORT:

- Offer your support; ask for the customer's commitment.

- Promise what you can live up to; live up to what you promise.

CLASS is not a sales script. There are no "magical" statements to memorize, no "surefire" techniques to use on the customer. CLASS does have its own language and flow, however, of compassion, patience, and simplicity.

All of these "techniques" are grounded in the approach described earlier in *The Tao of Sales*, Chapters 1-21. Used in that spirit, they can be powerful; used in the intention to force a sale on the customer, they easily backfire—not because the technique is flawed but because the intention is harmful.

All these techniques gain power through solid preparation. The more you know about the customer's business, the more directed your questions can be about areas of real potential opportunity. The more you know about how your products and services have helped other customers, the more helpful you'll be in tailoring what you sell to this specific customer's needs. See Chapter 43-49 for ways to develop this preparation.

It's all about creating mutual trust over time.

FLOW THROUGH ALL RELATIONSHIPS, business and professional, as simply as possible, with compassion and patience. Harmonize the feelings within yourself so you can make a gift of that harmony to others.

4

FIRE
Open your heart
Discover and act on
the best possible
"Win/Win"
commitment

3

5

WOOD
Open your eyes
See like a "mirror"
that reflects all the reality in the situation—
"good" and "bad"

EARTH
Open your spirit
Choose to serve some
purpose larger than
yourself

*Open Your
Life*

*Start
Breathing*

WATER
Open your ears
Hear everything
without judging
anything

2

METAL
Open your mind
Start discovering:
stop controlling

1

Notes

A TRUE STORY

Experiences just like this, hundreds of them, led to the search for "simple selling" and the writing of this book. There has to be an easier way, and it starts with rethinking the whole process and purpose of selling.

The customer is a fish.

That is, according to the advice we get from most popular sales-training literature. We are told that our job as salespeople is to *hook the prospect,* and then to *hold* that person's interest as we outline the reasons for purchasing our products and services. And when we're not fishing, other manuals advise us to *fight* to *win* the customer's order. That's selling the hard way

Candace Deasy, who runs her own training company, the Renaissance Company, tells the story of walking down a corridor in a hospital some years ago with a doctor she knew. Suddenly the doctor grabbed her arm and pulled her into a store room. "What's wrong?" she exclaimed. "It's one of those drug reps," he exclaimed. "I can't stand to listen to his spiel one more time. Let's wait a minute or two here, then you go out and see if the coast is clear."

Another doctor told her: "Drug reps are easy to get rid of. I nod politely without listening, and say 'yes' to their obvious questions, especially the last one, 'Will you prescribe Drug X to your next five patients?' Then they leave and I can go back to work. They believe my 'yes' means 'yes.' It really means 'go away.'"

A PERSONAL JOURNEY

xiii   *Zen Buddhism* (Mount Vernon, NY: Peter Pauper Press, 1959), p. 31.
        Compare this Sufi story from *The Way of the Sufi,* Idries Shah (New York: Penguin Books, 1974), p. 207:

> One went to the door of the Beloved and knocked. A voice asked: "Who is there?"
> He answered: "It is I."
> The voice said: "There is no room here for me and thee."
> The door was shut.
> After a year of solitude and deprivation this man returned to the door of the Beloved. He knocked.
> A voice from within asked: "Who is there?"
> The man said: "It is Thou."
> The door was opened for him.

This is the central issue: are the relationships you establish with customers "I-it" relationships (to use Martin Buber's terms), in which customers exist for your satisfaction and accomplishment, or "I-thou" relationships in which the goal is mutual well-being? Are you selling merely to make money, or to make a difference for others and yourself? For one thoughtful businessman's response to this question, see Tom Chappell, *The Soul of a Business* (New York: Bantam Books, 1994), p. 12 ff., and especially p. 23, "The Board of Directors Meets Martin Buber."

xiv   "When people see..." *Tao Te Ching*, tr. Stephen Mitchell (New York: Harper Perennial, 1988), p. 2.

"Success is as hollow..." Mitchell, p. 13.

xv   "Fill your bowl..." Mitchell, p. 9.

"In dwelling, live close to the ground..." Mitchell, p. 8.

xvii   "The sage is never opinionated..." *Tao Te Ching*, tr. Man-Ho Kwok, Martin Palmer, and Jay Ramsay (Rockport, MA: Element Books, 1993), p. 49.

xviii   "What is built on rock..." Kwok, Palmer, and Ramsay, p. 54.

"The Master sees things as they are..." Mitchell, p. 28.

"The mark of a moderate man..." Mitchell, p. 59.

xix   "The Tao gives birth to all beings..." Mitchell, p. 51.

xx   "I have just three things to teach..." Mitchell, p. 67.

xxi   "The Master does his job..." Mitchell, p. 30.

FINDING WITHOUT LOOKING

2   If you read a translation that has the Chinese calligraphy, like Gia-Fu Feng and Jane English's or Man-Ho Kwok, Martin Palmer, and Jack Ramsay's, you'll note the repetition of the figure 道 for "tao" in the first seven characters. Same word, different meanings; same meaning, different words.

Stephen Mitchell's translation of the first chapter of the *Tao Te Ching* makes clear the rich complexity and transparency of the Tao. "The tao that can be 'tao-ed' (expressed) is not the eternal Tao. The name that can be named is not the eternal Name" (p.86). The word "Tao" means "way," as in a street name, or a path, or a spiritual process. It also means "truth," how things really happen. It can be used to mean "the right way," but for a Taoist the "right" way includes the "wrong" way, just as rain can create both flowers and floods. Mitchell adds, "Other possible renderings: 'The way that can be weighed/ is not the eternal Way,' 'The force that can be forced/is not the eternal force' " (p. 86).

3   Thich Nhat Hanh, in *Peace is Every Step*, writes: "Defiled or immaculate. Dirty or pure. These are concepts we form in our mind. A beautiful rose we have just cut and placed in our vase is pure. It smells so fresh, so good. A garbage can is the opposite. It smells horrible and is filled with rotten things. But that is only when we look on the surface. If we look more deeply we will see that in just five or six days, the rose will become part of the

garbage. And if we look into the garbage can, we see that in a few months its contents can be transformed into lovely vegetables, and even a rose" (*Peace is Every Step* [New York: Bantam Books, 1991], pp. 96-97).

4   Robert Fritz, *The Path of Least Resistance: Learning to Become the Creative Force in Your Own Life* (New York: Fawcett Columbine, 1984), p. 21. This book explores the question of inner versus outer direction for one's life. Fritz shows how our upbringing in society can condition us to believe that power and reality exist outside ourselves, and thus our happiness depends on our ability to respond to this external power or react against it in the belief that rebellion against external forces constitutes freedom.

> One way or another, most people believe circumstances are the driving force in their life. When circumstances are central to your life, you may feel you have only two types of choices: either to respond to the circumstances or react against the circumstances. You can be either the "fair-haired boy" or the "last angry man" (*The Path of Least Resistance,* p. 18).

The Tao teaches that both of these responses, in effect, our "flight" and "fight" responses to the stress we perceive in our lives, imprison us in a world of unhappy dependency and knee-jerk anger. Freedom and happiness exist, on the other hand, in the choice to be fully ourselves, in harmony with the peaceful spirit of how things happen naturally.

Given the popularity of Stephen Covey's *The Seven Habits of Highly Effective People* (New York: Simon & Schuster, Fireside Books, 1990), one would think the only working-aged people who haven't heard of it have been living in a cave. Its strength is its combination of practicality and spirituality, at the same time. That's a combination all of us could learn to develop in ourselves. If you haven't done so already, buy it, read it, do it. A good place to start is with Covey's "Habit 1: Be Proactive."

> Look at the word responsibility—response-ability—the ability to choose your response. Highly proactive people recognize that responsibility. They do not blame circumstances, conditions, or conditioning for their behavior. Their behavior is a product of their own conscious choice, based on values, rather than a product of their conditions, based on feelings (p. 70).

6   John Heider, *The Tao of Leadership: Leadership Strategies for a New Age* (New York: Bantam Books, 1985), p. 9. This is a simple, splendid book about finding, developing, and living by the spiritual source of true leadership. It is as faithful to the original spirit of the *Tao Te Ching* as it is immediately, powerfully applicable to the confusion of today's world.

> Natural law is blind, its justice evenhanded. The consequences of one's behavior are inescapable. Being human is no excuse.
> The wise leader does not try to protect people from them-

selves. The light of awareness shines equally on what is pleasant and unpleasant.

People are not better than the rest of creation. The same principle which underlies human beings underlies everything equally.

One person is as worthy as the rest. Why play favorites? (*The Tao of Leadership*, p.9).

Peter Block uses an exercise in his Staff Consulting Skills Workshop in which people are asked to identify someone who makes them feel angry or powerless, and then find one thing about this person which they can personally value and respect. The exercise is to practice giving this person the positive feedback, simply, sincerely, with no disclaimers or "but"s. The learning comes when you actually do it and feel the potential for change open up in what has been a difficult or blocked relationship.

7   Neil Rackham, in *Spin Selling* (New York: McGraw-Hill, 1988), describes the results of ten years studying over 35,000 salespeople, looking for the behaviors characteristic of the very best, most successful salespersons. In high-value, complex sales, he found that most of the techniques taught and practiced in traditional selling not only weren't used by the top salespeople, they actually produced more resistance, more objections, and more reluctance to close in customers.

One of his surveys asked this question of professional buyers: "If you detect that a seller is using closing techniques while selling to you, what effect, if any, does this have on your likelihood of buying?" (*Spin Selling*, p. 35). The results:

More likely to buy	(4 percent)
Indifferent	(33 percent)
Less likely to buy	(63 percent)

Of course, we know this from our own experience without needing the evidence of the survey. We don't like being used, especially by a salesperson who cares more for his own gain than our well-being.

What does work, in his analysis? Not merely "closing a sale," but "opening a relationship" in which the customer is able to achieve significant goals as a result of buying the sales rep's products and services.

The point of selling, therefore, is to discover these goals, and help customers understand the value and urgency of acting to achieve them. Some sales trainers I talk with who like Rackham's book are concerned that his emphasis on the difference between successful approaches in large and small sales makes it hard to apply his methodology to their specific markets. Others believe he places too little emphasis on the importance of developing trust-based relationships before getting deeply into the sales process. If selling is based on an open exchange of information, then creating the rapport that allows for that reasonably open dialogue is critical.

147

These concerns are legitimate. I personally find the "SPIN" methodology somewhat artificial and inflexible. But Rackham has made a huge contribution to understanding how the buying decision really takes place and how salespeople need to work with customers in influencing that decision in positive ways. Salespeople, managers, or executives who still believe selling is something you have to do **to** customers must read this book.

8   Burton Hall is a highly-successful media consultant who lives, daily, with his clients, the kind of values this story exemplifies.

John Heider: "Keep in mind that 'Tao' means how: how things happen. But 'how-things-happen' is not the same as 'what-should-I-do?' No one can tell you what to do. That is your freedom. That is your responsibility" (*The Tao of Leadership*, p. 145).

9   Ever since Dr. Herbert Benson first pointed out, decades ago, the role of relaxation and meditation in stress reduction and heart disease, people have been waking up to the notion that our physical bodies are inextricably interconnected with both mind and spirit.

What we're starting to learn is the depth of this interconnection that links us not only with healthy personal well-being, but with the healing spirit present in the entire universe.

Books on relaxation and meditation fill the shelves of book stores. *Focusing,* by Eugene T. Gendlin, Ph.D., was one I used when I first started meditating, but it's a simple process. Better to do it than read about it. *Peace is Every Step* works just fine, too. Part One, "Breathe! You Are Alive," is the place to start:

> Our breathing is the link between our body and our mind. Sometimes our mind is thinking of one thing and our body is doing another, and mind and body are not unified. By concentrating on our breathing, "In" and "Out," we bring body and mind back together, and become whole again (*Peace is Every Step* [New York: Bantam Books, 1991], p. 9).

Another useful place to start is Diane Dreher's chapter, "Releasing Tension," in *The Tao of Inner Peace* (New York: HarperCollins, 1991). The chapter contains several approaches to restoring a sense of inner balance. "Taoist exercise can restore our inner harmony, returning the rhythms of our lives to more natural patterns" (p. 76).

Willis Harman, President of The Institute of Noetic Sciences, has conclusively shown, in *Higher Creativity: Liberating the Unconscious for Breakthrough Insights,* how relaxed meditation plays a central and centering role in creative breakthroughs. Check out his last chapters on dream-work, as well as the exercises following the section on Creating in this book starting at page 81.

11   The breakthrough step in interpersonal conflict is to realize that there are
two people involved. Two people share the responsibility for the conflict; two
people are needed to resolve it, but one person, yourself, can start the process
of reconciliation by changing the things you do that nourish the conflict.

The Appendix to Charles Johnston's *Necessary Wisdom* describes how
you can create an internal dialogue in which you view conflict situations of
any kind from both perspectives in order to find a healing approach. It's
simple. It works. See Johnson, p. 235 ff.

In chapter 10 of *The Fifth Discipline*, "Mental Models," Peter Senge
describes Chris Argyris' "Left-Hand Column" technique of understanding
and clarifying the hidden assumptions that cloud understanding between
people and fuel conflict. Another simple, useful tool. (*The Fifth Discipline*
[New York, Doubleday, 1990], pp. 195-202).

In his note to chapter 8, Stephen Mitchell quotes his teacher Emilie
Conrad-Da'oud, the founder of Continuum.

> Water is the source of all life, life's matrix and fecundity; it over-
> flows into everything, it moves everywhere. We are fundamen-
> tally water: muscled water. And the idea that we ever leave the
> amniotic fluid is a misconception. The amniotic fluid is the
> state of total nourishment and unconditional love. It is always
> present for us and contains everything we could possibly want.
> In fact we are that fluid of love (Mitchell, *Tao Te Ching* [New
> York: Harper Perennial, 1988], p. 89).

13   "In dwelling..." *Tao Te Ching,* tr. Gia Fu Feng and Jane English, (New
York: Random House, 1972), p. 13.

16   "The Master Nan-in..." This Zen story has been told countless times, probably in all the languages people speak. I encountered it first in *Zen
Buddhism*, (Mount Vernon, NY: Peter Pauper Press, 1959), p. 30. Paul Reps
includes it as the first story in his *Zen Flesh, Zen Bones* (Boston and Tokyo:
Charles E. Tuttle, 1957), p. 19.

Scott Peck, in *A World Waiting to Be Born*, talks about this quality of
"emptiness" and our reluctance to trust the quiet within us.

> This process of emptying the mind is ... not an easy process.
> Despite the fact that mystics through the ages have extolled the
> virtues of emptiness, people are generally quite terrified by it. It
> may help to remember, therefore, that the purpose of emptying
> the mind is not ultimately to have nothing there; rather it is to
> make room in the mind for something new, something unex-
> pected, to come in. What is this something new? It is the voice
> of God. (*A World Waiting to Be Born* [New York: Bantam Books,
> 1993], p. 88).

17   A whole methodology has grown up around the practice of observing and "mirroring" people, called "Neuro-Linguistic Program." A deft practice as well as an ugly name. One of the most accessible books on the subject as well as the most ethical is Genie LaBorde's *Influencing With Integrity*. In fact, many of us are so self-absorbed that we notice almost nothing about the people we work with, or, for that matter, the people we live with. Our lack of awareness turns them into flat, two-dimensional cardboard cutouts. Learning to observe people "in depth" is a powerful, graceful art, so long as the motivation behind it is "no harm."

20   The skills in this section are easy to practice anywhere, in any of our relationships. In fact, it's probably better to develop confidence in them in situations which don't carry the self-imposed pressure of a sales call. Spend three or four days in which you look for opportunities to use other people's language in your own speech, to ask people to expand on their ideas, or to replace "Yes, BUT..." with "Yes, AND." Notice the immediate effect this kind of sharing has on other people.

21   Another well-known, well-loved Zen story. John Conger, of the Pingry School, told it to me in the 60's. It took me many years before I realized that his point was that I was carrying around the burden, not the people I was upset at. It appears in *Zen Flesh, Zen Bones* as "Muddy Road" (p. 33), and in *Zen Buddhism* (p. 41).

22   Eugen Herrigel, *Zen in the Art of Archery* (New York: Vintage Books, 1971), pp. 33–34. This book is a moving account of the encounter between the Western and Eastern minds. The valuable lessons from the book for me are that the internal struggle to effortlessly "go with the flow" is part of the learning, and that I cannot demand or require insight, only accept it. I quote from it frequently in this book because of the joy and good sense it expresses.

BECOMING CENTERED

23   Peter Vail, in *Managing as a Performing Art* (San Francisco: Jossey-Bass, 1989), devotes his first chapter, "Permanent White Water," to an analysis of both the turbulent times we live in and the need to develop an appropriate personal and organizational style to navigate through these times.

> Perhaps even the metaphor of permanent white water is not adequate; we are not talking merely about a wild river; we are talking about an unpredictable wild river.... Things are only very partially under control, yet the effective navigator of the rapids is not behaving randomly or aimlessly. Intelligence, experience, and skill are being exercised, albeit in ways that we hardly know how to perceive, let alone describe (*Managing as a Performing Art,* pp. 2-3).

24   "The archer, competing...." My version of a story by Chuang Tzu which I discovered in Benjamin Hoff's *The Te of Piglet* (New York: E.P. Dutton, Penguin Books, 1992), p. 110. Hoff's goal in *The Tao of Pooh* and the *Te of Piglet* has been to "release Taoist wisdom from the grip of the Overacademics and restore to it the childlike awareness and sense of humor that they had taken away."

25   "Immersed in the wonder..." *Tao Te Ching*, tr. Stephen Mitchell (New York: Harper Perennial, 1988), p.16.

28   *A Course in Miracles*: (Mill Valley, CA: Foundation for Inner Peace, 1975), p. 319. This book is a simple, eloquent spiritual guide built on principles that Lao Tsu would have completely understood and honored. We get to choose what kind of world we live in: one of abundance and love or scarcity and fear.

     Thich Nhat Hanh on anger: "When our anger is placed under the lamp of mindfulness, it immediately begins to lose some of its destructive nature. We can say to ourselves, 'Breathing in, I know that anger is in me. Breathing out, I know that I am my anger.' If we follow our breathing closely while we identify and mindfully observe our anger, it can no longer monopolize our consciousness" (*Peace is Every Step* [New York: Bantam Books, 1991], p. 57). The whole chapter, "Mindfulness of Anger," is essential reading.

     I've worked with many women sales professionals who struggle with what are very "masculine" metaphors and approaches for selling. One of them recommended that I read Harriet Goldhor Lerner's *The Dance of Intimacy* and *The Dance of Anger*. They're wise, sensitive, absolutely straightforward books that women and men involved in relationships (business or personal) would benefit from reading.

     "Don't 'should' on me...." David Roth writes and performs wonderful "folk" songs that consistently invite listeners to re-think the assumptions built on hate and fear, and re-discover the joy and love that waits patiently within all relationships. If you skipped over the title to "Don't 'should' on me and I won't 'should' on you" without reading it aloud, do so now. Get it?

29   "From the viewpoint..." Frederick Franck, *A Compendium on that Which Matters* (New York: St. Martin's Press, 1993), p. 28. Franck, author of *The Zen of Seeing*, wrote a tough, loving book called *A Little Compendium on That Which Matters*. It's worth reading because it's so disturbing, in the same way disturbance in a stagnant pool stirs up again the regenerative life within that pool: "Where the Dow replaces the Tao, all of Life becomes desecrated" (*A Little Compendium*, p. 52).

30   Tom Chappell, *The Soul of a Business* (New York: Bantam, 1994), p. 94.

     Stephen R. Covey, *The Seven Habits of Highly Effective People* (New York: Simon & Schuster, Fireside Books, 1990), pp. 108 and 88.

31 From Peter Senge, *The Fifth Discipline* (New York: Doubleday, 1990). *The Fifth Discipline* is not the easiest read in the world. To understand why it's worth reading, even at the rate of a chapter a month (or a year), start with chapter 2, "Does Your Organization Have a Learning Disability," and ask yourself, "Do I have a learning disability that will keep me stuck in a way of life that is rapidly disappearing?"

Then read chapter 4, "The Laws of the Fifth Discipline," and think about how you currently interrelate with customers or clients. (pp. 57-67.)

1. Today's problems come from yesterday's "solutions."
2. The harder you push, the harder the system pushes back.
3. Behavior grows better before it grows worse. (Curing the symptom doesn't cure the disease, and certainly doesn't foster "health.")
4. The easy way out usually leads back in. (When you apply the same old solution to problems, you get the same old results.)
5. The cure can be worse than the disease.
6. Faster is slower.
7. Cause and effect are not closely related in time and space. (The actions we take today impact others miles and years away.)
8. Small changes can produce big results—(if they operate on fundamental leverage and aren't merely one more knee-jerk reaction) but the areas of the highest leverage are often the least obvious.
9. You can have your cake and eat it too—but not at once. ("Either-or" thinking is seductive, because it tempts us with the notion that we have "done something" about a problem. Better results, however, happen when we look for the long-term gains from "both-and.")
10. Dividing an elephant in half does not produce two small elephants. (His point is based on the story of "the blind men and the elephant," in which several blind men, encountering an elephant for the first time, and touching only the part of the elephant they bump into, argue fruitlessly over their perceptions. "An 'elephant' is like a tree trunk." "No. An 'elephant' is like a great spear." "You're both wrong. An 'elephant' is like a gigantic boa constrictor." Knowing the "whole elephant" means not only seeing complex issues in their entirety, but understanding how separate parts work together in the whole.)
11. There is no blame. As the Tao says, "Failure is an opportunity. If you blame someone else, there is no end to the blame." Mitchell, *Tao Te Ching* (New York: Harper Perennial, 1988), p 79.

NON-DOING

34 Tom Robbins, *Another Roadside Attraction* (New York: Bantam Books, 1990), pp. 133–4.

35 Consider also John Heider: "The less I make of myself, the more I am" (*The Tao of Leadership*, p. 43).

37 Another Sufi story, "The Door":
Salih Qazwin taught his disciples:
"Whoever knocks at the door continually, it will be opened to him."
Rabia, hearing him one day, said:
"How long will you say: 'It will be opened'? The door has never been shut" (Idries Shah, *The Way of the Sufi* [New York: Penguin, 1974], p. 240).

38 "There was something…" *Tao Te Ching*, tr. Stephen Mitchell (New York: Harper Perennial, 1988), p. 25

39 Margaret Wheatley, *Leadership and the New Science* (San Franciso: Barrett-Koehler, 1992), p. 34. This book has been rightly described as "The best, most lucid new thinking of any of the 'Leadership books' to come out in the past few years," by James Autry, author of *Love and Profit*, himself no slouch when it comes to lucid thinking and writing. Ken Blanchard was equally impressed. "A book like *Leadership and the New Science* only comes along once a decade." Her premise is simple: our business (and political) institutions, and the larger economy in which they operate, are based on 17th-century scientific assumptions about the world that emerged from the breakup of the medieval world some 250 to 400 years ago. "Reason" is "good." "Control" is "good." "Logic" is "good." "Imagination" is "bad." "Chaos" is "bad." "Creativity" is "bad." And spirituality belongs in churches, not in the whole life of people. As Alexander Pope put it in 1732, "Know then thyself; presume not God to scan. The proper study of mankind is man." From this we constructed a mechanistic view of the universe, as a gigantic machine, fueled by inexhaustible natural resources, existing for the benefit of mankind (white males, actually).

    As Joel Barker so frequently reminds us, we are now going through a "paradigm shift" like the one that spawned this earlier view of the universe and our role in it. Just as "science" in the 1500's to 1700's "called all in doubt," so now, scientific breakthroughs are demonstrating that the controlled and controllable world we believed in doesn't work that way at all. What's "real" is chaos. What's also "real" is our ability to experience and act on patterns of order that grow directly out of what we perceive as "chaos." We gain understanding of these patterns through clear values and open communication, not control. We gain power and purposefulness by participating in these patterns, not fighting against them. How Taoist.

40 Mel Ziegler, *The Republic of Tea* (New York: Bantam Doubleday Dell, 1994), p. 51. Another extraordinary testimony to the value of combining smart business sense with loving "life" sense. As *Inc.* magazine put it: "This new book is a gem. The idea is inspired." Even Tom Peters is lucid on Mel and

Patricia Ziegler and Bill Rosensweig's creative odyssey that led to the formation of the company, Tom's of Maine. "The *Republic of Tea* could well change your entire vision of what business—business as life, life as business—can be."

41   Another Sufi story, "Why the Dog Could Not Drink":
Shibli was asked:
"Who guided you in the Path?"
He said: "A dog. One day I saw him, almost dead with thirst, standing by the water's edge.
"Every time he looked at his reflection in the water he was frightened, and withdrew, because he thought it was another dog.
"Finally, such was his necessity, he cast away fear and leapt into the water; at which the 'other dog' vanished.
"The dog found that the obstacle, which was himself, the barrier between him and what he sought, melted away.
"In this same way my own obstacle vanished, when I knew that it was what I took to be my own self. And my Way was first shown to me by the behavior of—a dog" (Idries Shah, *The Way of the Sufi* [New York: Penguin, 1974], p. 185).

42   Mel Ziegler on "Not-doing":

"Not-doing," I learned, was listening to what wants to happen by itself, not forcing it, not attempting to control, but only serving it by helping remove the obstacles that are keeping it from happening (*The Republic of Tea*, p. 241).

WIN/WIN

46   Meyerson's account appears in "Everything I thought I knew about leadership is wrong," *Fast Company*, April:May, 1996, p. 71. A great article in a magazine that approaches today's business with a healthy dose of both hope and skepticism.

"There is a time..." *Tao Te Ching*, tr. Stephen Mitchell (New York: Harper Perennial, 1988), p. 29.

48   "Weapons are the tools..." Mitchell, p. 31.

49   "If powerful men..." Mitchell, p. 32.

"The warrior...." My version. See Thomas Cleary's *Zen Antics* (Boston: Shambhala, 1993), p. 11.

51   Margaret Wheatley, *Leadership and the New Science* (San Franciso: Barrett-Koehler, 1992), p. 39.

52   "A successful general...." My adaptation from the Taoist *The Art of War*.
      The original appears in Thomas Cleary's translation (*The Essential Tao*, p.
      91). The whole book is a very useful tool for anyone running a business in
      today's world. Note, for example: "If the leaders can be humane and just,
      sharing both the gains and the troubles of the people, then the troops will
      be loyal and naturally identify with the interests of the leadership" (p. 44).

No Struggle

56   Alan Watts and Ranier Maria Rilke: Both these references appear in Charles
      Johnston's *Necessary Wisdom* (Seattle: ICD Press, 1991) pp. 13, 39, another
      "essential book" in translating Taoist thinking into the everyday language of
      work and relationships. The "necessary wisdom" he describes is the ability
      to "bridge" the differences we experience between ourselves and others (for
      example, our clients, our managers, our spouses and loved ones, our children,
      our parents) without seeking either to deny them or obliterate them.

57   "In time the soft..." John Heider, the *Tao of Leadership* (New York: Bantam
      Books, 1985), p. 71.

      "In battle, combat is engaged...." *The Art of War*, my adaptation. (See also
      Cleary's translation of Sun Tzu, *The Art of War* [Boston: Shambhala, 1993],
      pp. 94-95.)

      Practicing oppposites: Jenny Behr points out: "Doing 'opposites' seems to
      violate the principle of rapport: demonstrating affinity with people, allow-
      ing them to have their point of view without arguing against them, 'mir-
      roring' their energy. 'Opposites' seem to work better when you have taken
      the time to develop empathy, and when they are used to invite people to
      work with you creatively, not push them away."

60   John Heider: "Since all creation is a whole, separateness is an illusion. Like
      it or not, we are all team players. Power comes through cooperation, inde-
      pendence through service, and a greater self through selflessness" (*Tao of
      Leadership*), p 39.

63   Thich Nhat Hanh on "Duality":

         When we want to understand something, we cannot just stand
         outside and observe it. We have to enter deeply into it and be
         one with it in order to really understand. [Literally, "Stand
         under."] If we want to understand a person, we have to feel his
         feelings, suffer his sufferings, and enjoy his joy.... In Buddhism,
         we call this understanding 'non-duality.' Not two (*Peace is Every
         Step* [New York: Bantam Books, 1991], p. 100).

      Not mind. Not Buddha. But also two. No two flowers are the same, or peo-
      ple. But also one. And therefore three.

                                    155

64   In his note to chapter 16, Mitchell quotes Lin Ching-hsi:

> A mirror will reflect all things perfectly, whether beautiful or ugly; it never refuses to show a thing, nor does it retain the thing after it is gone. The mind should be as open as this. (*Tao Te Ching* [New York: Harper Perennial, 1988], p. 93).

66   Stephen R. Covey *The Seven Habits of Highly Effective People* (New York: Simon & Schuster, Fireside Books, 1990), p. 79.

Timothy Gallwey, *Inner Skiing* (Toronto: Bantam Books, 1977, p. 134). *Inner Skiing* and *Inner Tennis* are all about how to "do" Taoist "non-doing."

SERVICE

67   Karl Albrecht's *At America's Service* makes good sense of what service means from an organizational perspective. If you're running or working in a company, and have decided to make service your dominant competitive and operational principle, read this book. Then, if you haven't done so already, read Peter Block's *Stewardship,* especially the last few chapters.

70   The original "SERVQUAL" (RATER) categories came from the research of Leonard Berry (*Marketing Services, Competing Through Quality*, and *Delivering Quality Service*). I have modified the original categories to reflect a service process in which service is done "with" customers and not merely "for" them.
      I asked the leadership group of one client, PR Newswire, consisting of 30 home office, field, and technical support managers, to define what excellent service meant to them as an organization, using the "RATER" categories. Here's their answer:

> In an atmosphere of mutual respect:
> - Be accurate and truthful with everyone
> - Listen: Hear, translate, communicate understanding
> - Understand and communicate expectations and results
> - Be responsible: Take ownership of results in situations— say No when appropriate
> - Promptness—get it done in time
> - Commit to knowing the client's business
> - Listen to customer needs and directions
> - Act with understanding that you are responsible
> - Seek out the necessary knowledge and skills to learn and improve
> - Be flexible in meeting and managing other's expectations

Their story of trusting these values under great competitive pressure appears in this book on pages 77–79.

74   "I am kind...." *Tao Te Ching*, tr. Kwok, Palmer, and Ramsay (Rockport, MA: Element Books, 1993), p. 1

CREATING

85   "Everything is created...." *Tao Te Ching*, tr. Kwok, Palmer, and Ramsay (Rockport, MA: Element Books, 1993), p. 129.

86   *A Course in Miracles*: (Mill Valley, CA: Foundation for Inner Peace, 1975), pp. 6 and 157.

Thich Nhat Hanh again:

> There are many kinds of seeds in us, both good and bad. Some were planted during our lifetime, and some were transmitted by our parents, our ancestors, and our society.... Our ancestors and our parents have given us seeds of joy, peace, and happiness as well as seeds of sorrow, anger, and so on. Every time we practice mindful living, we plant healthy seeds and strengthen the healthy seeds already in us (*Peace in Every Step* [New York: Bantam Books, 1991], p. 74.

87   "When the court is...." *Tao Te Ching,* tr. Gia Fu Feng and Jane English, (New York: Random House, 1972), p. 53.

Mel Ziegler, *The Republic of Tea* (New York: Bantam Doubleday Dell, 1994) p. 172.

88   Robert Fritz, *The Path of Least Resistance* (New York: Fawcett Columbine, 1984), p. 31.

90   Marv Weisbord and Sandra Janoff, in their Future Search Conference approach, have helped thousands of people unleash the creative power that comes from designing a desired, ideal future, and then working backward from it to the present state of things. Their experience with this approach, working with groups of up to 100 people at a time, is described in *Discovering Common Ground and Community Building: Renewing Spirit & Learning in Business*. A detailed discussion of the process itself appears in their latest book, *Future Search: An Action Guide to Finding Common Ground in Organizations & Communities*.

> We are convinced that acting out our dreams as if we *are living them now* [my italics] contributes greatly to widespread implementation. We have dozens of reports of this phenomenon from many sectors. We believe it reflects a practical embodiment of our assumption that mind and body are one (*Future Search* [San Francisco: Berrett-Koehler, 1995], p. 91).

For yet another example of creativity in action, read chapter 6 of *The Soul of a Business*, "Inspiring and Managing Creativity," pp. 106 ff.

91   Stephen Mitchell, *Tao Te Ching*, note to chapter 16 (New York: Harper Perennial, 1988), p. 93.

92   All of the exercises in *The Tao of Inner Peace* by Diane Dheher (New York: Harper Perennial, 1991) are practical, common sense, and also very spiritual ways of gaining depth in our lives. In regard to creativity, note especially the exercises in Dreher's chapter 12, "Natural Harmony." (pp. 121 ff.)

See also Dreher's exercise in guided meditation on p. 194 in chapter 18 of *The Tao of Inner Peace*: "The sense of oneness with all creation can best be achieved through meditation or contemplation, which awakens our powers of intuition. Our intellect analyzes and separates reality into logical categories, but the Tao transcends reason. Like water, it contains tremendous strength. It nurtures, but cannot be grasped."

94   Margaret Wheatley, *Leadership and the New Science* (San Franciso: Barrett-Koehler, 1992), p. 23.

One "breakthrough" tool for individuals or groups is "mind mapping," first developed by Tony Buzan. A description of mind-mapping in large groups occurs in *Future Search*. The mind map for *The Republic of Tea* appears opposite page 21 in that book. See also Senge's discussion in *The Fifth Discipline* (New York: Doubleday, 1990), p. 281.

There are lots of ways to open one's mind to the Tao ("how things work") of the natural world. In the introduction I mentioned *Leadership and the New Science, The Dancing Wu Li Masters,* and *The Tao of Physics.* Another, insight appears in Alan Watts' in *The Tao of Philosophy*, chapter 8, "Seeing Through the Net":

> In the history of philosophy, poetry and art [and of course business], we find the interaction of two personality types which I call "prickles" and "goo." The prickly people are advocates of intellectual porcupinism. They want a rigor with very precise statistics and they have a certain clipped attitude in their voices. They accuse other people of being disgustingly vague, miasmic, and mystical. However the vague, miasmic, and mystical people accuse the prickly people of being mere skeletons with no flesh on their bones. They say, "You just rattle. You are not really a human being. You know the words but you don't know the music." So therefore, if you belong to the prickly type, you hope that the ultimate constituent of matter is particles. [Logic, male, rational, left brain, control, Yang]. If you belong to the gooey type [of personality] you hope it is waves. [Intuition, female, creative, right brain, flow, Yin].... Yet we know well that this natural universe is neither prickles nor goo exclusively. It is gooey prickles and prickly goo, depending on your level

of magnification (*The Tao of Philosophy* [Boston & Tokyo: Charles E. Tuttle, 1995], p. 81).

John Heider called Alan Watts a "cultured rascal." What a compliment.

95   Jeanne Borei and John Pehrson, "Enter the Shadow," in *Community Building*, (San Francisco: New Leaders Press, 1995), p. 404.

LEADING BY FOLLOWING

96   Peter Block, *Stewardship: Choosing Service Over Self-Interest* (San Francisco: Barrett-Koehler, 1993), p. 42.

Peter Block's books and speeches have contributed powerfully to the lives of thousands of executives, managers, and employees. The particular power of *Stewardship* is its challenge to ground business success in spiritual values, rather than the "military" values of paternalistic control, organizational consistency, and predictable outcomes that have dominated business since the start. "There is a longing in each of us to invest in things that matter, and to have the organization in which we work be successful. One of [the book's] goals is to quicken our efforts to reform our organizations so that our democracy thrives, our spirit is answered, and our ability to serve customers in the broadest sense is guaranteed" (p. 3).

John Heider: "Good leadership consists of doing less and being more." (*Tao of Leadership* [NewYork: Bantam Books, 1985], p. 113)

99   "If you can govern...." *Tao Te Ching*, tr. Kwok, Palmer, and Ramsay (Rockport, MA: Element Books, 1993), p. 142.

100   "The mark of...." *Tao Te Ching*, tr. Stephen Mitchell (New York: Harper Perennial, 1988), p.59.

101   "Governing a large...." Mitchell, p. 60.

Sun Tzu, *The Art of War,* tr. Thomas Cleary (Boston: Shambhala, 1988), p. 47.

104   Margaret Wheatley, *Leadership and the New Science* (San Franciso: Barrett-Koehler, 1992), p. 104.

105   Mel Ziegler: "I firmly believe that if you have to do business, then you should do it without complaint, without ambivalence, with full mind and heart, as best you can—never allowing yourself to forget why you are doing it. That way the 'how,' not the 'what,' drives the business and you don't get lost" (*The Republic of Tea* [New York: Bantam, Doubleday, Dell, 1994], p. 174).

"Simplify actions to a few concrete principles." I've been working with a regional retail client that has a very ambitious goal: to expand into a national organization and take the privately-held company public. One of my first actions with them was to invite the top leadership group of about 25 people to create and then follow their own "organizational code of conduct," and to live with the challenges, opportunities, joy, and stress that results from making that kind of bold choice.

After the first six months of making the commitment and working together to implement it, here's what they had to say:

> "Communication is much better on the District Store Manager and Warehouse level. Where there used to be tension—an 'us vs. them' mentality—we realize we are part of the same team with the same challenge. There's a spirit of cooperation with my boss, our team, and the store that was never there before. The teamwork allows us to make good decisions about how to allocate products to the area where they will have the greatest market impact. We couldn't have done that before."

> "As managers and supervisors, we're taking more time to go out of our way to listen to people and explain our positions. We explore problems with employees ahead of time instead of saying 'do it my way.' In February, I really didn't think it could happen, but the DM's are actually using this stuff in the stores."

> "There's more of an 'ask' and less of a 'demand' atmosphere. We listen to each other instead of blaming and trying to get things done our way."

> "Now that we know how to communicate person to person, we're impatient for the computer systems that will make that communication even more efficient."

> "Our core group of senior managers learned we could listen to each other, be more tolerant of each other, and solve problems and act on opportunities better and faster. There's a committed effort to the company's success that just wasn't there before."

> "We go to the source of the problem now instead of carrying everything to top management."

> "Now when a key person is sick or on vacation, everybody pitches in to make sure the crises stay under control and the work gets done. Before, it was chaos."

> "My efficiency as a merchandiser is much greater. I get better information faster. When there are problems, I know it's okay to give the problem back to the person who owns it rather than

just trying to do it myself. I'll help, if I can, but they can carry out their responsibility."

In the twelve months since this work started, their profits have steadily grown at a rate double the industry's.

107 Wheatley, *Leadership and the New Science*, p. 116.

108 Carl Japiske, *The Tao of Meow* (Alpharetta, GA: Enthea Press, 1990), p. 101.

109 For a discussion of the Taoist approach to "dualities" like "male and female," "action and feeling," or "hard and soft" as business and life principles, try chapter 10, "Exploring Your Dualities: Yin and Yang," in *The Tao of Inner Peace*, (p. 99 ff.) or Johnston's chapter 4 in *Necessary Wisdom*, "You and Me: Loving as Whole People." (p. 39 ff.)

ENTREPRENEURIAL TAO

111 Throughout this book, I have noted examples of successful entrepreneurs, large and small, who have had the boldness to build their business on the basis principles and profit. At a time when large companies seem mindlessly bent on destroying both, and themselves in the bargain, examples like these I mention are heartening. But, I think, the challenge is not merely to applaud (or envy) what Tom Chappell, or the Zieglers and Bill Rosensweig, or any of another thousand companies have done. Nor is the challenge to imitate them, although one can certainly learn from them.

113 "One day a poor farmer's son...." Yet another classic, which also appears in Mitchell's note to chapter 74 (*Tao Te Ching* [New York: Harper Perennial, 1988], p. 109).

The guidelines for running a "Learning Organization," appear in Senge, chapter 12, "Team Learning" (*The Fifth Discipline* [New York: Doubleday, 1990], pp. 233). His source is David Bohm's concept of "Dialogue" (p. 238 ff.). The whole chapter is worth reading.

114 "If a leader is closed-minded..." my adaptation. In Cleary, *Zen Antics, publication data* p. 5.

118 Eugen Herrigel, *Zen in the Art of Archery* (New York: Vintage Books), p. 70.

119 In the jacket notes describing Paul Hawken's *The Ecology of Commerce*, from which the information in this extract was adapted, Fritjof Capra, author of *The Tao of Physics*, says, "This is, in my view, the first extensive, truly ecological analysis of business; deeply disturbing and yet full of hope. Essential reading for all who care about our planet." George Gendron, Editor-in-Chief of *Inc.* magazine, adds, "This book, like the vision of capitalism it describes, is gentle, healing, restorative, and quietly eloquent. It will not

make you richer, smarter, or more charismatic. It will merely challenge you to reexamine everything you believe about how business is currently practiced, how we create meaning in our lives, and the fabric of the legacy we are weaving for our children."

Hawken says:

> We have to recognize that we've reached a watershed in the economy, a point at which "growth" and profitability will be increasingly derived from the abatement of environmental degradation, the furthering of ecological restoration, and the mimicking of natural systems of production and consumption. The purpose ... is to end industrialism as we know it. Industrialism is over, in fact; the question remains how we organize the economy that follows.
>
> Either it falls in on us and crushes civilization, or we reconstruct it and unleash the imagination of a more sustainable future into our daily acts of commerce (*The Ecology of Commerce*, [New York: Harper Business, 1993], pp. 210-212).

Paul Hawken is both visionary and absolutely, toughly practical. Anyone starting a business would benefit from his book *Growing a Business*. In *The Ecology of Commerce*, note his principles for "sustainable" businesses:

- Replace nationally and internationally produced items with products created locally and regionally;
- Take responsibility for the effects they have on the natural world;
- Do not require exotic sources of capital in order to develop and grow;
- Engage in production processes that are human, worthy, dignified, and intrinsically satisfying;
- Create objects of durability and long-term utility whose ultimate use or disposition will not be harmful to future generations;
- Change consumers to customers through education."
  (*The Ecology of Commerce*, p. 144 ff.)

120 See also Tom Chappell's *The Soul of a Business*: "We believe that the company can be financially successful, environmentally sensitive, and socially responsible." Not a safe bet, not a sure thing. Just a clear choice. Then read "How to Create Diversity and Honor It—In Yourself and Others" (*The Soul of a Business* [New York: Bantam Books, 1994], pp. 152-3).

If I had to select only one book for new entrepreneurs to read for the "how to's" of marketing and selling, Levinson's *Guerrilla Marketing Excellence* would be it. The title is engagingly misleading. It's tough and principled at the same time.

"Guerrilla Marketing's Golden Rule #12: Do everything in your power to employ marketing techniques and tactics that are honest above reproach" (*Guerrilla Marketing Excellence* [Boston: Houghton Mifflin, 1993], p. 45).

MASTERY

122 "My teachings are easy...." *Tao Te Ching*, tr. Stephen Mitchell (New York: Harper Perennial, 1988), p. .

124 Timothy Gallwey talks about his experiences in helping people forget what they "know" in order to concentrate on what they are doing in the moment.

> "How can I forget what I know?" demanded an irritated trial lawyer from New York.... You can't forget what you know, but you can forget what you think you know—that is concepts, images and beliefs. When you do, all that's left is what you really know (Timothy Gallwey and Bob Kriegel, *Inner Skiing* [Toronto: Bantam Books, 1977], p. 134).

125 "Therefore the Master...." Mitchell, p. 72.

Eugen Herrigel, *Zen in the Art of Archery* (New York: Vintage Books), p. 73.

126 I asked Joe Masterson how he distinguishes among the people he offers help and support to. Clearly, some people reciprocate and some don't. Some understand that "one hand washes the other," and some just take for themselves. "Start simply," he said, "but give them something they can immediately use. A name, an idea, a resource. Then wait a month and see if they come back to you, at least with a 'thank you.' The people you want to work with will sort themselves out."

128 Peter Block, *Stewardship* (San Francisco: Barrett-Koehler, 1993), p. 18.

129 "A student...." *Zen Buddhism* (New York: Peter Pauper Press, 1959), p. 32.

130 "What kind of person is it...." *Tao Te Ching*, tr. Kwok, Palmer, and Ramsay (Rockport, MA: Element Books, 1993), p. 183.

Now, from the same verse, in Mitchell's translation:

> *As it acts in the world, the Tao*
> *is like the bending of a bow.*
> *The top is bent downward;*
> *the bottom is bent up.*
> *It adjusts excess and deficiency*
> *so that there is perfect balance (p. 77).*

Then Gia-Fu Feng and Jane English:

The Tao of heaven is like the bending of a bow.
The high is lowered, the low is raised.
If the string is too long, it is shortened;
If there is not enough it is made longer. (p. 77)

Then Eugen Herrigel:

We master archers say: one shot—one life! What this means, you cannot yet understand. But perhaps another image will help you, which expresses the same experience. We master archers say: with the upper end of the bow the archer pierces the sky, on the lower end, as though attached by a thread, hangs the earth. If the shot is loosed with a jerk there is a danger of the thread snapping. For purposeful and violent people the rift becomes final, and they are left in the awful center between heaven and earth (*Zen in the Art of Archery,* p. 35).

131 Eugen Herrigel:

You already know that you should not grieve over bad shots; learn not to rejoice over the good ones. You must free yourself from the buffeting of pleasure and pain, and learn to rise above them in easy equanimity, to rejoice as though not you but another had shot well. This, too, you must practice unceasing-ly—you cannot conceive how important it is (*Zen in the Art of Archery,* p. 69).

"Failure is an opportunity...." Mitchell, p. 79.

"If you want...." John Heider, *The Tao of Leadership* (New York: Bantam Books, 1985), p. 159.

132 Block, *Stewardship,* p. 231.

Bibliography

EDITIONS OF THE TAO TE CHING
AND OTHER ORIGINAL TEXTS

Tao Te Ching. Translated with an introduction by D.C. Lau. New York: Penguin Books, 1963.

Tao Te Ching. Translated by Gia-Fu Feng and Jane English. New York: Random House, 1972.

Tao Te Ching. Translated with an introduction by Man-Ho Kwok, Martin Palmer, and Jay Ramsay. Rockport, MA: Element Inc., 1993.

Tao Te Ching. Translated with an introduction and commentary by Stephen Mitchell. New York: Harper Perennial, 1988.

Te-Tao Ching. Translated with an introduction and commentary by Robert G. Henricks. New York: Ballantine Books, 1989.

Cleary, Thomas. *The Essential Tao: An Initiation into the Heart of Taoism Through the Authentic Tao Te Ching and the Inner Teachings of Chuang-tzu*. San Francisco: HarperCollins Paperback, 1991.

Sun Tzu: *The Art of War*. Translated with an introduction by Thomas Cleary. Boston: Shambhala, 1988.

Zen Antics: A Hundred Stories of Enlightenment. Translated and edited by Thomas Cleary. Boston: Shambhala, 1993.

Zen Buddhism. Mount Vernon, New York: The Peter Pauper Press, 1959.

Zen Flesh, Zen Bones: A Collection of Zen and Pre-Zen Writings. Transcribed by Nyogen Senzaki and Paul Reps. Boston and Tokyo: Charles E. Tuttle Co., 1957.

COMMENTARY

Cleary, Thomas. *Rational Zen: The Mind of Dogen Zenji*. Boston: Shambhala, 1993.

Dreher, Diane. *The Tao of Inner Peace*. New York: HarperCollins Publishers, Inc., 1991.

Franck, Frederick. *A Little Compendium on That Which Matters*. New York: St. Martin's Press, 1993.

Hanh, Thich Nhat. *Peace is Every Step*. New York: Bantam Books, 1991.

Heider, John. *The Tao of Leadership*. New York: Bantam Books, 1985.

Herrigel, Eugen. *Zen in the Art of Archery*. New York: Vintage Books, 1971.

Rajneesh, Bhagwan Shree. *Tao: The Three Treasures*. Poona, India: Rajneesh Foundation, 1976.

Shah, Idries. *The Way of the Sufi*. New York: Penguin Books, 1974.

Watts, Alan. *The Tao of Philosophy: The Edited Transcripts*. Rutland, VT and Tokyo: Charles E. Tuttle Co., 1995.

Watts, Alan and Chung-liang Huang, Al. *Tao: The Watercourse Way*. New York: Pantheon Books, 1975.

OTHER SOURCES

A Course in Miracles: (Mill Valley, CA: Foundation for Inner Peace, 1975)

Albrecht, Karl. *At America's Service.* New York: Warner Books, 1992.

Block, Peter. *Stewardship: Choosing Service Over Self-Interest.* San Francisco: Berrett-Koehler Publishers, Inc., 1993.

Capra, Fritjof. *The Tao of Physics.* Berkeley, CA: Shambala, 1975.

Chappell, Tom. *The Soul of a Business.* New York: Bantam Books, 1994.

Covey, Stephen R. *The Seven Habits of Highly Effective People.* New York: Simon & Schuster, Fireside Books Edition, 1990.

Edelman, Joel and Mary Beth Crain. *The Tao of Negotiation: How You Can Prevent, Resolve and Transcend Conflict in Work and Everyday Life.* New York: HarperCollins Publishers, Inc., 1993.

Franck, Frederick. *A Little Compendium on that Which Matters.* New York: St. Martin's Press, 1993.

————. *The Zen of Seeing.*

Fritz, Robert. *The Path of Least Resistance.* New York: Fawcett Columbine, 1984, 1989.

Gallwey, Timothy and Kriegel, Bob. *Inner Skiing.* Toronto: Bantam Books, 1977.

Gozdz, Kazimerz, ed. *Community Building: Renewing Spirit & Learning in Business.* San Francisco: New Leaders Press, 1995.

Harman, Willis, and Rheingold, Howard. *Higher Creativity: Liberating the Unconscious for Breakthrough Insights.* Los Angeles: Jeremy P. Tarcher, Inc., distributed by St. Martin's Press: New York, 1984.

Hawken, Paul. *The Ecology of Commerce.* New York: Harper Business, 1993.

————. *Growing a Business.*

Herrmann, Ned. *The Creative Brain.* North Carolina: Brain Books: The Ned Herrmann Group, 1989.

Hoff, Benjamin. *The Te of Piglet.* New York: E. P. Dutton & Co. Inc., Penguin Books, 1992.

Japiske, Carl. *The Tao of Meow.* Alpharetta, GA: Enthea Press, 1990.

Johnston, Charles M., MD. *Necessary Wisdom.* Seattle: ICD Press, 1991.

Laborde, Genie Z. *Influencing with Integrity.* Palo Alto, CA: Syntony Publishing, 1983.

Lerner, Ph.D., Harriet Goldhor. *The Dance of Anger.* New York: Harper & Row, Publishers, 1985.

————. *The Dance of Intimacy.* New York: Harper & Row, Publishers, 1989.

Levinson, Jay Conrad. *Guerrilla Marketing Excellence: The Fifty Golden Rules for Small-business Success.* New York: Houghton Mifflin Company, 1993.

Morgan, Gareth. *Imaginization.* Newbury Park, CA: SAGE Publications, Inc., 1993.

Peck, M.D., M. Scott. *A World Waiting To Be Born.* New York: Bantam Books, 1993.

Rackham, Neil. *Spin Selling.* New York: McGraw-Hill Book Company, 1988.

Senge, Peter M. *The Fifth Discipline.* New York: Doubleday Currency, 1990.

Vaill, Peter B. *Managing as a Performing Art.* San Francisco: Jossey-Bass Publishers, 1989.

Wheatley, Margaret J. *Leadership and the New Science.* San Francisco: Berrett-Koehler Publishers Inc., 1992.

Weisbord, Marvin, and Sandra Janoff. *Discovering Common Ground: How Future Search Conferences Bring People Together to Achieve Breakthrough Innovation, Empowerment, Shared Vision, and Collaborative Action.* San Francisco: Berrett-Koehler, 1992.

———. *Future Search: An Action Guide to Finding Common Ground in Organizations and Communities.* San Francisco, Barrett-Koehler, 1995.

Ziegler, Mel, Patricia Ziegler, and Bill Rosenzweig. *The Republic of Tea.* New York: Bantam Doubleday Dell Publishing Group, 1994.

Zukav, Gary. *The Dancing Wu Li Masters.* New York: William Morrow and Company Inc., 1979.

LITERARY ACKNOWLEDGMENTS

*Exerpted material in this work has been been reprinted by
kind permission of the following. All rights reserved.*

Reprinted by permission of Doubleday, a division of Bantam Doubleday Dell Publishing Group Inc.: Tom Chappell, *The Soul of a Business* (New York: Bantam, 1994); Thich Nhat Hanh, *Peace in Every Step* [New York: Bantam Books, 1991]; John Heider, *The Tao of Leadership.* New York: Bantam Books, 1985.Tom Robbins, *Another Roadside Attraction* (New York: Bantam Books, 1990); Senge, Peter M. *The Fifth Discipline.* (New York: Doubleday Currency, 1990); Mel Ziegler, *The Republic of Tea* (New York: Bantam Doubleday Dell, 1994)

Reprinted with permission of the publisher: *Stewardship: Choosing Service Over Self-Interest ,* © 1993 Peter Block; *Leadership and the New Science,* © 1992 Margaret Wheatley. Berrett-Koehler Publishers, Inc., San Francisco, CA. All rights reserved.

Reprinted with the permission of HarperCollins Publishers, Inc: material from *The Ecology of Commerce,* by Paul Hawken. © *1993 by* Paul Hawken; *Tao Te Ching,* Stephen Mitchell, tr. © 1988 Stephen Mitchell.

Reprinted by kind permission of the publisher: Alan Watts, *The Tao of Philosophy* © *1995 Mark Watts* Boston & Tokyo: Charles E. Tuttle Co., Inc. an imprint of Periplus Editions, HK.

The quotations on pages 28 and 86 are from the text, pages 319, 6, and 157, of *A Course in Miracles®* © Copyright 1975, Reprinted by Permission of the Foundation for Inner Peace, Inc., P.O. Box 598, Mill Valley, CA 94942.

Reprinted with the permission of Simon & Schuster: material from *The Seven Habits of Highly Effective People* by Stephen R. Covey. Copyright © 1989 Stephen R. Covey.

From *A Little Compendium on that Which Matters*, by Frederick Franck, copyright © 1993 by Frederick Franck. Reprinted by permission of St. Martin's Press Incorporated.

Reprinted with the permission of Random House: material from *Zen in the Art of Archery*, by Eugen Herrigel. © 1971 by Eugen Herrigel.

Reprinted with the permission of Penguin Books: material from *The Way of the Sufi, by Idries Shah.* © 1974 by Idries Shah.